I Remember
AUGUSTA

I Remember
AUGUSTA

*A Stroll Down Memory and Magnolia Lanes
at America's Most Fascinating Golf Club.
Home of the Masters Tournament*

MIKE TOWLE

Cumberland House
Nashville, Tennessee

Published by Cumberland House Publishing, Inc., 431 Harding Industrial Drive, Nashville, TN 37211

Cover design by Gore Studio, Inc.
Cover photo by Jules Alexander
Text design by Mary Sanford

Library of Congress Cataloging-in-Publication Data
Towle, Mike.
    I remember Augusta : a stroll down memory and magnolia lanes
  at America's most fascinating golf club, home of the Masters
  Tournament / Mike Towle.
      p. cm.
    Includes index.
    ISBN 1-58182-079-8 (alk. paper)
      1. Augusta National Golf Club--History. 2. Masters Golf
  Tournament--History. 3. Golfers--Anecdotes. I. Title.

  GV969.A83 T69 2000
  796.352'06'075864--dc21

                                                           99-089653

Printed in the United States of America
1 2 3 4 5 6 7—05 04 03 02 01 00

To Mom and Dad

Contents

ACKNOWLEDGMENTS

Writing a book about Augusta National Golf Club and the Masters Tournament begins with my love for golf, and for that let me begin by thanking my parents, Bill and Anne Towle, for introducing me to golf at the age of eleven. I shot a 123 for my first nine-hole round, while playing with my patient dad, at Newport Country Club in Vermont. I was hooked even though I sliced—a lot. When I was afflicted with a case of the shanks, Mom and Dad splurged for a lesson that sort of straightened me out, and they generously drove me to the golf course every day I wanted to play, which was, well, almost every day. Then they gave me the keys to the station wagon so I, as team captain and the only licensed driver among team members, could drive our high school golf team to various matches and tournaments (Coach Chuck Pearce needed that drive time to devise team strategy and break up fights without having to worry about keeping his eyes on the road). Thanks,

Dad and Mom, for trusting in me and letting me enjoy the game without butting in with Little League parents' syndrome.

My first (and, so far, only) trip to Augusta and the Masters was afforded me via my stint as a sportswriter for the *Fort Worth Star-Telegram*. Bruce Raben, Ellen Thornley, and Steve Meyerhoff gave me "the car keys" so I could finally drive down Magnolia Lane with notebook and laptop in hand; and Gayln Wilkins helped show me around once I got there. Thanks, too, to *Golf World* editors Ron Coffman, Dick Taylor, Brett Avery, Jim Herre, Terry Galvin, Geoff Russell, Michael Arkush, Alan Tays, and Ron Sirak for further indulging my passion for reporting on golf. Ditto for Frank Deford, Van McKenzie, Vince Doria, Mark Godich, and Peter Alfano at *The National*; Al Barkow, Michael Corcoran, and John Poinier at *Golf Illustrated*; Tim Murphy at *Golf Shop Operations*; and Rich Skyzinski and Brett Avery (him again) at *USGA Golf Journal*.

Cumberland House publisher Ron Pitkin showed a willingness to expand his company's foray into golf books, to include this book and a companion work on Ben Hogan. Mary Sanford was steady as she went in editing this book, while Ed Curtis was always there for me to bounce ideas off.

Thanks go to the folks who, with minimal trepidation, allowed me to interview them on the record, in years past as well as more recently, for their thoughts and remembrances of Augusta National and the Masters Tournament: Sam Snead, Ken Green, Frank Chirkinian, Dave Kindred, Melanie Hauser, Nick Price, Ron Coffman, D. A. Weibring, Larry Mize, George Archer, Steve Melnyk, Ken Beck, Hord Hardin, Mark O'Meara, John Derr, Doug Sanders, Mike Donald, Scott Hoch, Curt Sampson, Tom Weiskopf, Frank Beard, Al Barkow, Gary Player, Steve Eubanks, Billy Joe Patton, Charles Coe, Dick Von Tacky, and Tommy Jacobs.

ACKNOWLEDGMENTS

As always, my wife, Holley, and son, Andrew, supported me superbly and stood by patiently while I sequestered myself to do this book.

INTRODUCTION

Anyone's first visit to Augusta National Golf Club during Masters Tournament week is an exercise in awe as much as it is shock. The awe is in viewing in person the full-color beauty of Augusta's luscious surroundings of green grass, azaleas, dogwoods, and the magnolias and pines, even more vivid than seen through the eye of CBS-TV; the shock is in getting a close-up look of impeccably manicured fairways much hillier and greens even more undulating than TV viewers can imagine. That's not to say that climbing ropes are necessary to ascend Augusta's eighteenth hole, but a rope tow to accommodate a rare winter snow could turn the venue into a nice little ski area.

Augusta National and the annual invitational golf tournament it serves up, and which came to be known as the Masters, has been around less than seventy years, but it seems longer. Augusta and the Masters have forged a connected legacy such that if you didn't know any better, you might believe that the game of golf was invented here. It wasn't, although an argument could be made that the modern-day sport of golf was. Contemporary golf is now an ongoing television series where green spray paint and blue dye in the water are a golf-course superintendent's standby ingredients for an enhanced production. That's the influence of Augusta National as seen in full bloom every April when the Masters Tournament is brought into the living rooms of hundreds of millions of households around the world. Aesthetics and floral beauty have become as much a part of golf course maintenance plans as monitoring turf growth, applying insecticides, installing proper drainage, and fixing bunkers. Golfer, television commentator, and course designer Tom Weiskopf refers to this as the Augusta Syndrome, whereby greens committees and supers are told by their bosses to take a good look at Augusta and make the same thing happen at their home course. Alas, let it be known that everything done at Augusta is centered around the two or three weeks surrounding Masters time, and that when Augusta takes off all of its Hollywood makeup and the crowds depart and Cinderella loses her glass slipper, the place turns back into something more akin to a Plain Jane. Of course, that refers only to the physical appearance of the golf course and not the classic design of the layout or the storied tournament history or the fascinating growth and power of the most secretive golf club membership that enthusiastically shrouds itself in privacy. It is those things, those real institutions, that make Augusta National and its Masters the most intriguing, joined-at-the-hip golf attractions in the world. Even Saint Andrew's gets the British Open only about once every seven years or so.

One thing that makes Augusta and the Masters so special

is its ability to take root in the consciousness of golfers and golf fans. Once you've seen the Masters, it's hard to get it out of your mind. It is totally unlike other major tournaments, which jump from course to course every year, making it tricky to connect the dots when trying to recount the details of great U.S. Open shots or British Open comebacks or PGA Championship upsets. Let's see now, was that a three-wood or four-wood that Corey Pavin hit to the eighteenth at Shinnecock, or was it Baltusrol? Quick, name the two venues at which Greg Norman won his two British Opens. Try this one on for size: Describe any three of the five finishing holes at Sahalee. Hint: Tiger Woods won the PGA there way back in . . . 1999. Now, switch gears back to Augusta, and please write a 100-word essay off the top of your head about what happened in the lengthening shadows of a late Sunday afternoon at Augusta's sixteenth hole in 1975. Even if you hadn't been born yet, chances are you know the story of Jack Nicklaus and the monster birdie putt he made there on his way to victory. That's the power of Augusta and its capacity to shape our memories, to the point where nocturnal dreams as well as daydreams bring the place to life for us 365 days out of the year (or, incidentally, exactly one day for each acre comprising the grounds on which Augusta National resides).

This work is a compilation of hundreds of the best memories of Augusta and the Masters, provided—in most cases firsthand to the author—by dozens of golfers, club members, writers, and fans who have been there and walked and/or golfed the sacred grounds of golf's most venerable venue. *I Remember Augusta* is part reverential and at times brutally honest to the point of being mildly critical. It is at all times, however, a different kind of history of the club and the tournament, told scattershot by people who know the place. An effort was made to include sources from different generations and walks of life to present a balanced look covering all of the decades. The result, hopefully, is a fresh sketch of Augusta National and the Masters that is as entertaining as it is informative, and as revelatory as it is respectful.

—*Mike Towle*

I Remember
AUGUSTA

THE MEN

He (Roberts) had guts, I'll tell you what. He wouldn't let any riffraff in there.

—SAM SNEAD

―――――

Augusta National Golf Club is one of the last bastions of the Old South, a secretive and highly private club with a membership of about three hundred, including dozens of the richest and most powerful CEO-types in the world. Some of their names are known: Jackson Stephens, Warren Buffet, Arnold Palmer. Most Americans know of one or two people who belong to Augusta, but the trick is in getting everybody together so that a membership list can be drawn up and shown to the world. That's the only way the public is ever going to get its hands on such a list, because there's no way that the keepers of the Augusta National flame are going to release that kind of information. Augusta's membership rolls are as well guarded as the president's nuclear launch codes, and nothing short of a well-aimed missile strike at the ground-zero intersection of Interstate 20 and

Augusta's Washington Road is going to get those names pried out of the hands of the Augusta poo-bahs.

The only names associated with Augusta National and the Masters you really need to know can be counted on two fingers: Bobby Jones and Clifford Roberts. If you have all five fingers, you can add Alister Mackenzie, Dwight Eisenhower, and choose between Hord Hardin and Jack Stephens for a fifth, but the buck still stops with Jones and Roberts. That's pretty amazing considering that both men have been dead for more than twenty years. It is their influence, their spirit, their dictates that live on—Jones with his eternal title of President in Perpetuity and Roberts in his cosmic role as resident curmudgeonly dictator.

Jones and Roberts put their heads, wallets and money-raising skills together in the early 1930s and carved a golf club and eighteen-hole golf course out of a 365-acre tract of Augusta land that had been a nursery known as the Fruitlands. Jones, who had just retired as the greatest amateur golfer in history, teamed with renowned Scottish architect Alister Mackenzie to design the course, while Roberts spearheaded the financing effort, using his Wall Street connections and milking Jones's name to raise the funds needed to build Augusta National. This was during the depression and money was short, but Jones and Roberts ultimately were able to complete the club, and it opened for play in 1933.

This was the Georgia golf club that Georgia native Jones had dreamed of as being his haven-away-from-home, and it was soon to be followed by the creation of an invitational tournament originally known as the

Annual Invitational Tournament. At Roberts's urging, the event's name was eventually changed to the Masters Tournament, and the rest as they say is history, albeit a colorful and extraordinary one.

⚊⚊⚊

Augusta National Golf Club cofounders **Clifford Roberts** *and Bobby Jones shared Jones's dream, which was to build a classic golf course in Georgia that combined everything good and wonderful that Jones had seen and experienced in a decade-plus as the greatest golfer in the world. When you think about Augusta National now, it's impossible to imagine it being anywhere else. In the 1976 book he wrote about Augusta National and the Masters Tournament, Roberts recalls that Jones's choice of Augusta over his hometown of Atlanta didn't sit well with a lot of folks:*

Although I was not surprised at Bob's willingness to locate his golf course in Augusta, several others were greatly disappointed, including some of his closest friends in Atlanta, who thought that his home city deserved first consideration. Some even went so far as to predict failure if an Augusta site should be chosen. But Bob knew Augusta was the better choice for winter golf, and he became impatient to get started so as to have a really private place to play the game he so greatly enjoyed. Whenever he played a round on one of the Augusta courses, or at any place outside Atlanta, he found himself playing what amounted to an exhibition match, with galleries that often numbered in the hundreds or even thousands.[1]

⚊⚊⚊

Curt Sampson, author of the 1998 book The Masters, *performed diligent research in digging up the history behind the construction of Augusta National. Sampson traveled to the city of Augusta a number of times to learn as much as he could about the history of the club and the course, and he met some fascinating people along the way. The result is one of the most meticulous and insightful looks at the history behind a golf course now commonly regarded as the most familiar golf venue in the world:*

I enjoyed talking to some of the old guys who built the course and are still there. That was a highlight for me. One of the most memorable moments for me came when I sat in this guy's auto-glass shop and talked to his uncle, Dan Williams, who was one of the course's builders back in the early 1930s. In fact, you can find him in the front of the book, where there's an epigraph that reads "I forgot everything I remember." It was fascinating to me that they were able to build the course on a dime during the depression, even though there were all these CEOs backing the club and who had survived the crash. These guys didn't want to spend any extra money on the damn golf course so far away from home, and keep in mind that 80 percent of these people were New Yorkers. They did this thing on the cheap, and then they wound up not paying a number of the contractors. But building a masterpiece like that for not much money and with mostly hand labor is a wonderful thing I think. I was interested, too, in (Alister) Mackenzie and Jones, and their interaction.

Although Augusta National Golf Club was conceived by Bobby Jones, he had plenty of design support from renowned Scotsman architect Dr. Alister Mackenzie, whose handiwork had also included Cypress Point. **Clifford Roberts** *wrote fondly of Mackenzie, who passed away a year after Augusta National opened but before he could get there to see his finished design being enjoyed by golfers:*

Best of all, he was an open-book type who came forth voluntarily with stories about incidents which provided the answers to questions one might wish to ask. I saw quite a bit of the good doctor and, in fact, went out of my way more than once in order to be with him. He was invariably entertaining, partly as the result of a calculated effort on his part to reminisce a bit or to tell a Scottish story. Then too, as often as not, he was hilariously amusing quite unintentionally. He spoke with a rich Scottish burr and punctuated his remarks with typical Scots exclamations. Let something occur that was just mildly unusual and the Doc would instantly come forth with a comment that was to him altogether normal, but that made the incident an unforgettable occasion for the rest of us.[2]

Arnold Palmer *paid his due respects to Roberts and Jones in his 1999 autobiography:*

Being friends with Clifford Roberts, I would discover, was like learning Augusta National's proper angles—it took time, but the friendship, when it evolved, would be a lasting and genuine one. I met Bob Jones there, too—by then far past his playing prime and only a year or so away from being stricken by the illness (syringomelia) that

A good share of Augusta's lore is represented here as Bobby Jones (right, with cane) presents Billy Joe Patton (left) with the low-amateur trophy for the 1954 Masters. Ben Hogan is to Patton's left and Sam Snead looks in, too. Snead defeated Hogan in a Masters playoff that year. (AP/Wide World Photos)

would rack his body and eventually force him to use a customized golf cart to get around the grounds to see players and meet people. Mr. Jones, as I called him from the outset, was as unfailingly polite and kind-spirited as anybody I ever met at Augusta. Perhaps because amateur golf had meant so much to him—he won the Grand Slam as an amateur in 1930 and then retired from the game, as he described it, before he "needed" to make money in order to play—Jones harbored a special affection for amateur champions who found their way to Augusta, treating each and every one like the special young men he thought they were, myself included.[3]

———

*Almost a generation older than Arnold Palmer, **Sam Snead** got a chance to play with Jones before the latter's illness forced him to give up the game. Snead offers this succinct appraisal of Jones's golf game and compares Jones to Jack Nicklaus, who once inspired Jones to say of him, "He plays a game with which I am not familiar":*

I played two exhibitions with Bobby Jones and one round at Augusta. He was a good driver of the ball and a good fairway-woods player. And he was probably the best putter of his era. But he wasn't as good with his long irons. Yet, Jack Nicklaus was never a great sand or wedge player. But he hit it a long way, and I think Jack was the best putter there ever was.

———

*Winning the Masters Tournament and the green jacket that goes
with it does not entitle one to play Augusta National on a
whim, nor does being a U.S. senator carry a lot of weight there.*
Sam Snead *explains, offering some insight into Clifford
Roberts's character as well:*

Roberts was a real stickler for the rules. One time Arnold
Palmer went down there with his dad (Deacon) to play
some golf. Roberts told Palmer that his dad couldn't play
unless he was playing with a member. There was another
time when a senator came down there accompanied by
someone to play with, and they just went out and played.
Someone went and told Roberts that this senator was
playing without a member in his group. Roberts stayed
around until the senator had finished his round, then
went up to the senator and said, "Mr. Senator, it's in our
by-laws that you have to play with a member here. Well,
now that you've played, don't bother coming back." He
(Roberts) had guts, I'll tell you what. He wouldn't let any
riffraff in there. A rule is a rule, and that is a rule that
made me feel good.

⸺

*Augusta National's membership does not comprise a democracy.
All major decisions are handled by a select few, or the one.
Layers of committees simply don't exist, and for that the members can thank or curse legendary sportswriter Grantland Rice,
one of the club's original members.* **Clifford Roberts** *recounts
what transpired to make Augusta's organizational structure different from most clubs':*

As club president, Bob Jones was anxious to take advantage of the opportunity to make a report on the club's funds, received and disbursed, and invited the members to attend a special dinner meeting for this purpose. After the dinner, Bob assembled his papers and called the meeting to order. But, before he could proceed, Grantland Rice was on his feet demanding to be heard. Grant explained that he had several times previously become a member of new clubs, all of which had gone broke. In looking back for a reason, he realized that all these promising new clubs, born of much enthusiasm, had made the mistake of holding a meeting, and he didn't want to see the Augusta National make this same mistake. Therefore, he proposed a resolution to the effect that Bob and Cliff be asked to run the club as they saw fit without the hindrance of meetings, and all who favored should stand and say, "Aye." Whereupon everyone stood and yelled, "Aye," and Bob could do nothing but join in the laughter and capitulate, despite his previously expressed determination, born of legal training, to conduct the club's business in proper fashion. The spirit of Grant Rice's resolution is still in effect, as the club's business has always been conducted with a minimum of formality.[4]

Herbert Warren Wind was the dean of American golf scribes for many years, and here he checks in with more words of praise for the Augusta cofounder who still reigns as the greatest amateur who has ever played the game:

As the most popular Southerner since Robert E. Lee and the most admired American athlete in the so-called Golden Age of Sport, (Jones) knew the best that life has to offer, and over the past twenty years he has known some of the worst. He has stood up to both situations with equal grace. He is the only person I know, in or out of sports, who has the Churchillian quality of being larger than life and at the same time intensely human and intimate. I love to be in his company and listen to him talk golf.[5]

—————

Frank Chirkinian for many years was CBS-TV's executive producer of golf, and together CBS and Chirkinian formed an association that played a significant role in elevating Augusta and the Masters to the heights of world renown it enjoys today. But CBS has never had carte blanche in producing its coverage of the Masters, and in the early years Chirkinian often found himself in Bobby Jones's presence for various briefings related to television coverage:

I learned a lot about golf coverage because of the Masters. In particular, I remember a meeting with Bobby Jones in my early years of covering the Masters. In fact, I got to know him very well, at least as best I could in a week's time on a yearly basis. He sat in his wheelchair and smoked. One day we sat for about two hours in his bedroom—him in his wheelchair and me sitting next to him. We talked about a lot of things that day. One of those things was that he never felt that money was pertinent to the outcome of a golf tournament. He always thought like an amateur golfer. He made the poignant observation that once the money was gone, the trophy and the memories would always remain. Money is irrelevant, so why talk about it (on the air)? That's why we never said one word about how much money is being played for in the Masters. Also, it's not really the championship of anything. It's not even a club championship. That's why we've never referred to the winner as the Masters *champion*. He's the tournament winner or the winner of the green coat.

The one thing that impressed me most about that meeting with Bobby Jones was his telling me, "Show your viewers as many golf shots as you can. That's why they've tuned in." We (CBS) have mastered that philosophy ever since . . . I still have a wonderful picture of the two of us with an inscription written by him in semi–chicken scratch. It must have taken him an hour to write one sentence. He wrote, "I hope I read correctly between the lines that you would like to keep this photograph." Bobby Jones was the warmest, kindest person I've ever met in my adult life. Everyone else comes in second. You know, he didn't like the idea of the tournament being called the Masters—that was Clifford Roberts's idea—but he finally gave in.

—◦◦◦—

Of all the U.S. chief executives who played golf, Dwight Eisenhower was the best known for his love of golf. Other presidents have been better golfers than Ike was, but none have had the honor of belonging to Augusta National as Eisenhower did. Ike wasn't just a token member, either. He and his wife,

15

Mamie, spent many weeks holed up in their Eisenhower Cabin on the grounds of the club. And the association went well beyond just member-club. **Clifford Roberts** *and other power-playing members of Augusta's inner circle were instrumental in not only convincing Ike to run for the presidency, but also for financing the infrastructure that led to his election in 1952. Roberts spoke well of the Eisenhowers as frequent guests at the club, making Augusta National Ike's golf version of Camp David:*

Ike fell in love with the place. He wanted to become a member—a full-fledged, dues-paying member. This was fortunate, because Bob and I had determined at the club's beginning not to have any honorary members. It was also most fortunate that Mamie liked the club just as much as Ike. This was difficult to understand, because she had no real interest in golf, and ours was essentially a man's club. Possibly the knowledge that Ike was happy and that she could be with him pleased her most of all. She thoroughly enjoyed the informal atmosphere.[6]

Writer and author **Steve Eubanks** *went where no man or woman had ever gone before when he authored his 1997 book* Augusta: Home of the Masters Tournament, *which offered a level of balanced candor never before seen in any book written about Augusta National and/or the Masters. Other book authors had fawned over Augusta and the Masters, while Eubanks didn't back off from exposing some of Augusta's warts. The difference was that while earlier authors didn't want to risk losing their Masters press badges, Eubanks was willing to take a chance—and he believes he lost his job because of it. It's a long* *story, but suffice it to say that Eubanks had been employed by someone with close ties to an Augusta member who in turn was mentioned in Eubanks's book for his part in a highly publicized controversy concerning racism in golf. When asked what fascinated him most about researching his book—the golf tournament or the political power plays behind the scene—Eubanks didn't hesitate in responding:*

It's the men behind the pretty golf course and golf tournament that fascinate me the most, because there is only so much about the golf course you can really talk about. It's very nice, it's pretty, and it's been there for more than sixty years. It's a wonderful place where a bunch of old guys can just get together and shank a lot without anyone seeing them. But when you start talking about the power and the influence and the number of those kinds of people that have come through there, and all of the things that went on while they were playing politics out there, that to me is the most intriguing part of the story. Before I wrote the book, I had always believed that the Eisenhower campaign was a grassroots groundswell that had built up by citizens standing with pitchforks out there drafting Eisenhower for president. As I began to research this and talked to historians and people who knew Clifford Roberts and who knew the other members of the gang, I found out the real story. This was not a case of a grassroots movement. Instead, it was almost a complete drafting by this small group of members who were very adept at making it look like a citizens-for-Eisenhower campaign. These guys are the ones who convinced Ike to run, put him out on the ballot, and made sure he got elected.

President Dwight Eisenhower spent a lot of his vacation time playing golf at Augusta. He even had a tree there named after him. (AP/Wide World Photos)

However, I'm not sure that the Augusta inner circle's political influence today is as much as it was back in the days of Eisenhower. The political spectrum is a lot different. In terms of the amount of wealth that is out there at the club, it is much greater than it has ever been, with guys like Warren Buffet on board. When you can turn down a Bill Gates, it really shows you what kind of power you are wielding. That's right: Bill Gates, the richest man in the world, could not get in. Part of the reason for that is that he lobbied to get in, and that's just not done at Augusta. The last thing you can let these guys know is that you actually want to join the club. That's almost the kiss of death. I think Bill will get in at some point—sometime after this little issue with the Justice Department is all squared away, and as long as he doesn't do any more television commercials. As long as he stays low-key about it, Gates will probably become a member after his fiftieth birthday. That seems to be sort of the threshold for when these guys get asked to join.

One other interesting thing that I found out is that Vernon Jordan, the black attorney and Bill Clinton's buddy, was on the list to replace the black member who got booted for lying to them about his résumé and other things he had done. They were left needing to fill his spot and thought it would be politically correct to have another black member out there. Jordan had been a frequent guest at Augusta and he seemed to get along with everyone well. But just as his name was being floated around the membership, the Monica Lewinsky story broke and that was dropped like a hot potato. He's done as far as being a member out there.

CBS-TV's **Frank Chirkinian** came to be known as "the Ayatollah," but even he had to answer to someone and it wasn't

19

always the brass at the network. For at least one week out of the year, Chirkinian's eagle-eyed boss was none other than Clifford Roberts. And Roberts ran a tight ship:

My most prominent memory of Clifford Roberts is the time I got my (butt) chewed out after one of my technicians drove a golf cart over Eisenhower's front lawn, even though it was actually part of the golf course. I was summarily called to his (Roberts's) office, where I got a very cold reception and a very hot reaming. It was a very spartan office . . . very plain . . . totally inelegant. There were two or three pictures on the wall, but nothing to make it a very personal place. There was not a piece of paper on his desk. He was intimidating, formidable. He was one crusty old man. It's fortunate that in my first two or three years of working the tournament, I was under a cloak of anonymity. Then my contact with him got a lot closer. Whenever there was a problem, I would get the phone call, and it was never his calling to say, "Have a nice day." Another time, I got chewed out for showing, on camera, a player cleaning his spikes. I remember it clearly: It was Bruce Devlin. When Cliff saw that, he made it clear to me that he would prefer a shot of the flowers behind the thirteenth tee to a player scraping dirt out of his spikes. You never really had much of a defense when it came to talking to Cliff.

—⸺⸺—

Chirkinian *goes further in his description of Roberts, almost to the point of describing the Masters Tournament chairman as obsessive-compulsive, or perhaps a micromanager:*

I think Cliff was the most meticulous human being that I've ever run into. For example, the club every year sends a gift to members of the media. One year it was a green leather-bound notebook for phone numbers and addresses. With the notepad came a typewritten note, mimeographed for everyone, that said, "When using this book, make sure you use a number-two pencil, sharpened." Not a number-three pencil; a number-two. I went ahead and used a number-three pencil, just to spite him.

---

*Golfer **Doug Sanders** saw a different side of Roberts:*

He was kinder than most people thought. I was a Georgia boy and I was *Yes, sir,* and *No, sir,* and all that. He couldn't have been any nicer. I didn't have any dealings with him except on a personal basis, and whenever he saw me it was "Hi, Doug." That made me feel good. The managers and everyone down there made me feel good. By the way, the wine room down there is one of the greatest in the world.

---

*Likewise, the late British golf writer **Peter Dobereiner** had words of praise for Roberts, who more often than not was the whipping boy when the critics aimed their arrows at Augusta, which wasn't often:*

To a large degree Roberts is not the ogre he pretends to be. The style of the man, as an uncompromising dictator, hides a natural shyness and a generous spirit. He has helped many people, in large and small ways, but always by stealth, covering his traces so well that as often as not his benefaction is not even suspected. If this austere old man commands respect rather than affection, then that is by his own choice, a sacrifice he has made in the cause of his beloved Masters.[7]

Roberts did have a sense of humor, as **Chirkinian** *can attest:*

As austere, autocratic, and mean-spirited as Roberts could be, he had a side to him that included a magnificent sense of humor. He had a great dry wit. It would come out in the kind of repartee that people just wouldn't expect from Cliff. I don't know if it's true or not, but there's a story of the time that he was in a bridge game with Ike as his partner. Ike was bidding for a grand slam without an ace in his hand. They were doubled and went down four, at which point Cliff said, "Mr. President, now you can understand why I can't let you run the country by yourself." He (Roberts) loved a good laugh, but he made sure he kept up a stern front. He was not an easy man to know.

Ike's pet peeve at Augusta was the tree at seventeen: He swore he was going to chop it down, only to get sternly rebuked by His Imperial Highness, who said, "If you touch that tree, you're a dead man, and not even the secret service will be able to help you."

Golfing great **Gary Player,** *who won three Masters Tournaments, endeared himself to both Bobby Jones and Clifford Roberts over time, and he probably came to know each club cofounder about as well as any golfer of his generation could:*

I spent a lot of time with Clifford Roberts and Bobby Jones. We used to have the international (golfers) dinner as well as the Masters Champions Dinner, and Bobby Jones was always there. I often had to cut his meat and light his cigarettes for him because of his rheumatism. He was a very, very fine man. We spoke about issues such as golf etiquette and how important this and the dress code was as well. One time I told him that whenever the flag on the third hole was put on the left side of the green, it was a very hard hole to birdie. He said, "Well, you're not supposed to birdie that hole. It's a par hole. In fact there are a lot of holes in golf that are designed to be par holes." That stuck in my mind as a young man.

I still have my first green jacket (from 1961) in my cupboard right here (at home in Johannesburg, South Africa). I'm ten yards from it right now. At the time, I didn't know that you weren't supposed to take the green jacket home. I brought it back home and one day my phone rings and it's Clifford Roberts in that stern voice of his asking me, "Have you taken your jacket home?" I said, "Yes, I have." And he said, "Well, nobody has ever done that and you're not supposed to do it." And I said, "Well, Mr. Roberts, why don't you just come and fetch it?" and he had a good chuckle about that. He then said, "Promise me that you'll never wear it in public and that you'll keep it in your cupboard." It's still right there alongside the blazers I have for other sports, and it sits right there with a plastic cover over it, and I never take it out of that plastic cover.

—⊶⊷—

Television golf commentator **Steve Melnyk** *was a topnotch amateur golfer back in the late 1960s and early 1970s, although an injury curtailed his career from going beyond the level of winning the U.S. Amateur. Melnyk got to play in the Masters Tournament as an amateur, and in turn had a chance to meet Clifford Roberts, even if it wasn't his first choice at that particular time:*

One of my favorite Clifford Roberts stories concerns the second year I played there. I came in early to play some practice rounds and was staying at the club. On the Saturday afternoon the week before the tournament, I got a call from Mr. Roberts's secretary asking me if I would like to join Mrs. Eisenhower, Mr. Nicklaus, and Mr. Roberts for dinner. I said, "I'm sorry, I can't go because I've already got plans." After I put the phone down, it rang again two minutes later. This time it was Mr. Roberts saying, "I'll meet you in the Trophy Room at 7:00 P.M. sharp." I guess I was just a little naive.

Mr. Roberts had a great sense of humor. He was incredibly bright but had a facade he liked to project. Later it got to where I kidded him, calling him "the Great Curmudgeon." I actually got to know him my first time there. Later I was selling insurance, traveling throughout the South. I would even call him when I was in the area, saying, "Mr. Roberts, I've got some business in Columbia (South Carolina, about fifty miles from Augusta), are you available to play some golf?" I was about twenty-two or twenty-three years old at the time, and he would set up a time for us to play at Augusta. I would play nine holes with Cliff. I must have played golf with him four or five times. We'd tee off at 2:00 P.M. and finish around 4:00 P.M. As soon as he stepped off the golf course and walked to the clubhouse, he would have fresh peaches waiting for him. He never had to order them—they just appeared.

⌘

*Roberts was not the only influential green jacket who had a say in how CBS-TV covered the Masters. As longtime CBS television and radio golf commentator **John Derr** learned, Bobby Jones also had a few ideas to contribute to the telecast:*

In 1955 we had bought the rights, and our first telecast of the Masters was to be in 1956. In the fall of 1955 our CBS producer, our engineers, and I went down to Augusta to determine where we were going to put the cameras. They had provided us with a station wagon and we had a chauffeur driving it. Mr. Jones offered to help us determine where the cameras would be located. They had never had television there, and they were a little afraid of it, not knowing what it might do to their attendance. Little did they know that it would bring crowds of people wanting to get in. That first year of television we had to black out everything from Charlotte to Atlanta because they didn't want to hurt the attendance.

Bob Jones ultimately decided where the cameras were to be placed. One thing he said was that he wanted a camera in the middle of the fairway, if we could get it. He wanted to see the shots that were required, what a man had to do, what was the challenge that he was faced with, such as if he were on the fifteenth hole: How far down the fairway off the tee did he have to be before he could try to go over the water and go for the green with his second shot? There were a lot of decisions to be made. I remember Bob saying, "You can have all the cameras on the green that you want, but basically all a camera on the green shows you is that if a round object gets struck it will roll."

In 1956, we put the cameras in place, although in those days we did only the last three and a half holes. Bob wanted that camera at fifteen as discussed so the second shot could be shown from behind. But the only way we could do that was to have a mobile camera that could be latched onto a tractor and moved out onto the fairway after players had hit their drives at fifteen. Then we would line up the camera behind them, and after they had hit their second shots, we would have to quickly get that tractor out of the fairway so that the next group could hit. And that's the way fifteen was covered in the first year. We didn't have any balloons overhead in those days—we had to use a dadgum tractor.

During the first Masters telecast, Derr and Roberts were surprised when they looked up to see who the leader on the scoreboard was—it was a golfer who would go on to become a legendary member of the CBS-TV golf crew. **Derr** *explains:*

That first year of television was experimental in so many ways. We didn't know what we were going to have, what we were going to get. I used to have tea with Cliff Roberts around ten o'clock every morning. And that first day we were sitting there at around eleven o'clock, when we looked down at one point and saw the big scoreboard down by the eighteenth hole. We noticed that this young amateur, a fellow by the name of Venturi, had birdied the first hole. Ken was there because he had been in the service in 1955 and had missed his opportunity to be there under his exemption earned from the year before, so he got a special invitation for 1956. He birdied the second hole and they put that up. He birdied the third hole and they put that up on the board. Cliff turns to me and says, "Well, Bob told me that we really needed to be covering all eighteen holes." Ken birdied the first four holes that day and shot 66.

Al Barkow, whose decades of golf-journalism experience included a stint with the Shell's Wonderful World of Golf *series, made his first visit to the Masters Tournament in 1969. It didn't take long for Clifford Roberts to make an impression on the young Barkow, and it wasn't necessarily a positive one:*

The first time I went to the Masters was in 1969. I went as a writer for *Golf* magazine that year, and I wrote a piece about Augusta and the Masters. In that article I was one of the first to get on their case as to why Charlie Sifford or no other black golfer had ever played there. That was the year Charlie had won in L.A. and had had a really good winter. He should have been there, but he wasn't.

There were very, very few articles in those days being written that were critical of Augusta and the Masters, and I took off on them. When I went down there the next year (1970), I remember seeing Herbert Warren Wind, a nice guy. He was connected with them, writing their film script every year for them. He wouldn't even be seen with me because he didn't want to get into trouble. And Bob Drum mentioned to me that Cliff Roberts had come out and asked, "Who's this Barkow guy?" I was fairly new to the business and had been with the *Shell's Wonderful World of Golf* show traveling around the world. I hadn't really been into the belly of the golf business.

That week in my second year there, I was doing a piece on Frank Chirkinian and how he worked. I went into the TV control truck from where Frank controlled the telecast, and there was one of Roberts's buddies sitting there in the room among a group of other people. Chirkinian introduces me to this guy, and the first thing he said was, "Er yewww the man who rut that article?" and then he tried to get me kicked out of the truck. That's when Chirkinian said, "He's doing an article on me—leave him alone."

So I was persona non grata after a couple of years, but I couldn't care less. It was always a good networking thing for me to be down there, when I was editor at *Golf Illustrated* it was important to see people and to be seen. It was a legitimate magazine, and we had a decent circulation, so they really couldn't refuse me.

All told I've been there about fifteen times. One thing about me is that I'm not a great Masters fan. I'm not enamored of the place and don't buy into all of the heavy adulations about Augusta. It's a very nice place and understated and all that stuff, but to me they're all just a bunch of damn hypocrites.

I really disliked Cliff Roberts a lot. I remember back again to my first Masters. There was some kind of press conference going on that Wednesday, and everyone was in this room waiting for Cliff Roberts to show up. All of a sudden there's this incredible hush, and I'm thinking, *Jeez, the pope is coming in.* So here comes this old guy with thick glasses who talked so softly and was so condescending. I said, "What the hell is all this? We're dealing with a golf tournament, not the Nobel Peace Prize or whatever." But still, when all is said, I like going down there because it's an interesting golf course and the play is always good.

If you're looking for romantic stuff about the place, I'm not the guy. I don't get it. I remember Tom Watson getting on Gary McCord's case for using a couple of phrases that I guarantee you none of those members even understood. I didn't even know what bikini wax was, and I'll betcha those old guys didn't, and they probably didn't even bother to ask. And Watson was carrying on, trying to get McCord fired and all that. It's like a plantation-boss thing. They're very rich guys and I would guess they wield a lot of financial power. They call it a major, but I never really thought of it that way because the field is never big enough. People are so taken with the place and it's always been a puzzle to me, although I'm not sure why.

*When **Jack Nicklaus** looked at Clifford Roberts, he didn't just
see a soft-speaking curmudgeon in glasses—he saw an innovator
when it came to golf and golf tournaments:*

Although Bob Jones was the inspiration for and, until his
death in 1971, the dominating presence at the Masters,
the man who did most of the work that built the tournament into golf's most glamorous occasion was Clifford
Roberts . . . The all-time supremo of the "benevolent dic-
tators" who have been the force behind so many of
America's finest pure golf clubs, Mr. Roberts liked to
have things his own way, and one of the things he was
always adamant about was the positioning of the holes
during the Masters. There were, Mr. Roberts insisted,
only four different cup locations on each green consis-
tent with the original Alister Mackenzie–Bob Jones
design plus later modifications. Although these surely
were mixed up from round to round, they were never
ever toughened or eased relative to what the fellows had
shot the previous day.[8]

---

*Roberts was adamant that all Augusta patrons wear proper
badges at all times, and there were no exceptions, as television
golf commentator and former golfer **Frank Beard** recalls with a
chuckle:*

One story I heard was the old Clifford Roberts story during the year when streaking was so popular. Clifford's big
deal down through the years were the season badges and
the season-badge list. He never wavered, and that's all he

ever talked about. When he was asked what he would do should a streaker go racing across the course on a Sunday, Roberts thought about it for a minute and then deadpanned, "I would take back his season badge." Those things are inherited through wills. I remember going to the tournament and trying to get tickets. I got them for my wife and kids, and that was it. One year my brother, his wife, and their son joined us there, and I couldn't get tickets for them, even when I offered to pay full price. All they said was "Sorry." And they know who's in your family and if you're trying to buy more than you should. One time they told me, "Your kids are six, five, three, and two—are they all going to be walking?" It became a battle, and it didn't matter what I said to them.

———

The club adopted a resolution in 1966 at its annual stockholders' meeting that paid tribute to Bobby Jones, who would die about five years later:

It has been well and truly said that "Every great institution is the lengthened shadow of a man." So it is with the Augusta National Golf Club: the man being Robert Tyre Jones Jr.

His was the established and unique leadership position coupled with remarkable ability, which was principally responsible for the organization and development of the Augusta National Golf Club and the Masters Tournament. He exemplifies the highest standards of sportsmanship and his position is pre-eminent throughout and beyond the golfing world.

Bob Jones, as he is affectionately known to his fellow

members, has served as President of the Augusta National Golf Club from its very beginning, being unanimously elected each succeeding year, and it is desired that the distinction of being the only President of the Club be preserved by changing the By-Laws so as to provide for his election as President in Perpetuity. More especially, it is desired that the spirit of his principles, his acts of good sportsmanship, his innate modesty, and other admirable and lovable qualities shall forever guide the policies of the Augusta National and the Masters Tournament.

NOW, THEREFORE, BE IT RESOLVED, That the By-Laws be amended to provide for the position of a President in Perpetuity as a lasting tribute to Robert Tyre Jones, Jr., and that he be the only person ever to be elected to that position.

RESOLVED, FURTHER, That the name of Robert Tyre Jones, Jr., President in Perpetuity, be carried on the letterhead and masthead of the Augusta National Golf Club as long as it continues in existence.

———

*While Bobby Jones was the greatest amateur golfer of the twentieth century, fellow Augusta member Charles Coe, of Oklahoma City, Oklahoma, has the greatest amateur record of all Masters contestants over the years. Included among his numerous high finishes is a tie for second with Arnold Palmer, a stroke behind Gary Player in 1961. **Frank Beard** remembers Coe as an integral part of Augusta and Masters lore:*

I remember shaking hands with Bobby Jones and meeting Clifford Roberts. But I didn't really have any interaction with either. Otherwise, I don't remember meeting an Augusta member except for Charlie Coe, a marvelous amateur golfer. One time I was the first one off for a Masters round and Charlie played with me as a playing marker. He was a great guy as well as a wonderful player. This was back in the days when many of the best players around still were amateurs—they weren't all turning pro at age nineteen or whatever like they do today. There was a lot of prestige to remaining amateur and winning the U.S. Amateur, which was then rated just a notch below the U.S. Open or the Masters in terms of prestige. It was something to be coveted. Charlie was an oilman from Oklahoma and one of about fifteen players of that era who chose to remain amateur.

Bobby Jones initiated the Masters in part as a tournament for amateurs because he himself had been an amateur for so long. His love was for the amateur game. But even early on this was a complaint heard at Augusta, a concern about the makeup of the field. Through the years, even today, it is known for having the weakest field of any major, even when you have the world's top twenty-five players in the field. There was a time when something like a third of the field was made up of amateurs. One year, with all the invitational criteria, they got the field up to about ninety players and Clifford Roberts about blew a gasket.

Any list of great men in Augusta National history would be incomplete without at least one mention of "the Squire." Gene Sarazen accomplished something that Jones or Roberts were unable to do without some outside help—put the Masters on the map. Sarazen gave the Masters its first big boost with his memorable double-eagle two at the fifteenth hole en route to winning the Masters in 1935. Sixty years later, Sarazen was still entertaining the Augusta patrons as one of the legends hitting the ceremonial first drive at the Masters. **Peter Jacobsen** *paid his respects to Sarazen in his 1993 book* Buried Lies:

It's fantastic that Gene Sarazen, this rare man who competed head-to-head with the likes of Walter Hagen and Bobby Jones and won all four major championships, is still active at ninety (as of 1993). I see Mr. Sarazen at least once a year, at the Masters.

Last year (1992) at Augusta, I was in the first twosome to play on Thursday, paired with Dillard Pruitt. When we walked onto the first tee, he (Sarazen) was seated chatting with Byron Nelson and Ken Venturi. Sarazen had hit the ceremonial drive off the first tee, and they were sort of holding court. Now, I proudly represent Toyota on the Tour, and as always I was wearing a Toyota visor. I shook hands with all of the legends, then Mr. Sarazen said (mainly for the benefit of the others), "How much do they pay you to wear that visor, a million bucks?"

His comment kind of took me back, but I just said, "I wish it was a million, Mr. Sarazen."

Then he turned around and jokingly said, "Aw, you young kids will put anything on your heads for the right price."

This, of course, got a wry laugh from the others, because when you're ninety years old and as well liked as Gene Sarazen, nearly anything you say is funny.

Although I was thinking that Toyotas didn't exist in his day or he certainly would have accepted their endorsement money, I walked over to my bag, took off my visor, and handed it to Mike (Cowan, Jacobsen's caddie). "Mr. Sarazen," I said, "out of respect for you, I will play this first hole without my visor."

He just chuckled, but Venturi winked at me, as though I'd done the right thing. I mean, what else could I have done?[9]

———

Hord Hardin was the second successor to Clifford Roberts as Masters chairman after Roberts committed suicide in 1978, and Hardin upheld the austere traditions of Augusta and the Masters in the best way he knew how, as **Gary McCord** *once attested to in a column of his that ran on iGolf:*

I spent the week preceding the Masters (McCord's first as an announcer, 1986) at a friend's house in Atlanta trying to seek spiritual enlightenment. All I got was a call from my wife telling me she was seeking a divorce. So much for the spirituality of the moment, hello alimony!

I was told to be at Augusta by Tuesday for a meeting with Hord Hardin, the tournament director. Frank (Chirkinian) was waiting patiently at our office for my arrival. We proceeded to Mr. Hardin's office; I felt like I was going to the principal's office. There was a look of concern on Frank's face as we went into the catacombs of the clubhouse at Augusta.

Hord Hardin met us in his dimly lit office. Bobby Jones artifacts were the main decor. It was musty with tradition. The conversation lasted about ten minutes. "We must maintain tradition, it is the cornerstone of the tournament," Mr. Hardin exclaimed. With some conversation on my part, I departed with the knowledge that Hord Hardin wasn't a bad host. He was a true debrouillard.

———

After Hardin retired, Arkansas billionaire Jackson Stephens took over as Masters chairman and learned quickly that almost everything he did was subject to public scrutiny, thanks to inquiring media minds of the likes of veteran golf writer **Melanie Hauser:**

I remember finding out after Tom Kite wasn't invited to the Masters one year (because he didn't meet the invitational criteria) that Stephens had written a letter to Tom—because he didn't qualify. I walked up to Jack Stephens and I asked him about the letter, and he was fairly surprised that I knew about it. There was kind of a little glint in the eye saying, "Hey, we just can't keep things away from you guys." It was kind of a funny way to approach it. Something he had done personally had been found out, and that surprised him.

THE MYSTIQUE

I was so nervous that my hands were shaking, and I had a hard time keeping the ball on the tee.

—LARRY MIZE

There is a powerful allure to Augusta National that involves beauty as much as it does intrigue. The beauty is in the magnolias, the azaleas, the dogwoods, and all the wonderful flora that grace the grounds of a golf club that for two or three weeks out of the year is the prettiest thing in America. It is an image fashioned out of aesthetics that have been carefully cultivated over the years, rendering a scene that is an art gallery as well as a venue for a very prestigious golf tournament. On the other end of the spectrum, well-known people have died at Augusta, one in particular by a self-inflicted gunshot wound. There are, figuratively speaking, elephants buried here, lending themselves to the surreal quality that makes up Augusta National. And if you don't believe the reference to the elephants, go take a good look at the undulations in the green at the fourteenth hole. Use your imagination.

Wishes can come true at Augusta, whether you're a golf fan determined to find the Holy Grail of golf, where pimiento sandwiches and Cokes in generic cups are sold on the cheap, or a professional golfer—or even a topnotch amateur one—looking to follow in the footsteps of a Gene Sarazen, a Ben Hogan, a Jack Nicklaus, a Tom Watson, a Nick Faldo, or a Tiger Woods. Augusta more than any other sports venue in the world has been privy to the thrill of victory (e.g., Nicklaus in '86) and the agony of defeat (Scott Hoch in '89 or Greg Norman in '84, or '86, or '87, or '96, or '99), and the emotions of both can still be felt and are renewed as new thrills and spills unfold almost every year at the Masters.

Ghosts of Masters past can be felt wafting through the towering trees of Augusta, and everywhere one turns, he or she can see some detail, some "custom," some golf-related innovation that is a leftover relic of the days of Bobby Jones and Clifford Roberts. Even today, Augusta officials steadfastly adhere to rules and customs established more than a half-century ago, rationalized by the mantra, "That's the way Mr. Roberts would have wanted it." Presidents and other world leaders have played golf here; high-ranking government officials have broken the rules here and been asked not to return. That is the influence and an outgrowth of the affluence of Augusta National, which more than any other sports institution is most often spoken of in religious terms usually associated with cathedrals and

Sunday church services. At Augusta, Mass is always in session.

―――

*The drive into Augusta National begins with a turn off mundane Washington Road onto gorgeous Magnolia Lane, where members, Masters participants, guests, and patrons alike literally enter a new world. Golfer **Frank Beard** competed in the Masters a number of times in the 1960s and 1970s, and not all of his goose bumps have disappeared:*

It's the most awe-inspiring feeling to drive into the golf club, play the golf course, and take part in the tournament. Anyone who can appreciate the roots of golf and the traditions, and has feelings for where golf came from—that the Bobby Jones–Walter Hagen era (of the 1920s) is when golf really began growing in popularity in the United States—knows what Augusta and the Masters means. It's a myth, but by that I don't mean it's a bunch of falsehoods. It's a believable, lovable myth. It's like going into one of those old caves exploring and seeing the writings and drawings on the walls from ancient times. You don't know if it's all true, but it sure is fun to be there and see it. I played there fourteen times. It was the most looked-forward-to event of the year.

―――

The breathtaking flora that grace the 365 acres comprising the grounds of Augusta National are not there by accident. The keepers of the club are well aware of exactly what is growing on their property, as was evidenced years ago by club cofounder **Clifford Roberts:**

Among the legacies the Augusta National inherited from the Berckmans family was the original importation into America of privet, which serves today as a hedge and remains in good condition. There are literally thousands of miles of privet hedge throughout the South which were propagated from this mother hedge. Another legacy is the wisteria vine *(Wisteria sinensis)* next to the clubhouse, which is recognized as the first wisteria to be established in this country. It is also believed to be the largest vine of its kind in the United States. A third inheritance are two live oak trees *(Quercus virginiana)* near the clubhouse, the age of which is estimated to be 250 years. Probably our most important possession of this type is the double row of Southern magnolia trees *(Magnolia grandiflora)*, which, as previously mentioned, line the 250-yard entrance driveway. A recent report furnished by an outstanding authority assures us that these sixty-five magnolia trees, if given the same care and attention they now receive, may be expected to live for another century and a half.[10]

———

Elements of mystery and intrigue have wafted their way through Augusta in the nearly seventy years it has been in existence, as once told by former CBS-TV executive producer of golf **Frank Chirkinian:**

There's a story I got second- or thirdhand about an oil-man named Jones who was killed in a plane crash with something like $2 million in a bag. Supposedly, the money was going to Ike to help for his retirement. I'm sure Cliff was behind all that, although I don't know whatever happened to the money.

——

*Another mysterious tale that has been told around Augusta is repeated here by former Masters winner **Sam Snead**, and it concerns the 1978 death of club cofounder Clifford Roberts, whose death has long been reported as being at his own hand. On the other hand . . .*

One of the stories that used to go around down there was that Roberts didn't shoot himself. Some of the waiters would say that they thought someone else shot him. After a while, though, things just faded away, and you don't hear anybody down there talking about it anymore. I don't know of anyone who didn't like Roberts.

——

*Augusta National and its Masters Tournament are not for everyone, as **Snead** points out:*

Moe Norman was invited to play there once. He played two holes and quit, saying, "I don't like it." There was another time when Jimmy Demaret was paired in the Masters with some guy who was getting ready to hit his ball, when he suddenly yelled, raised his club, and said,

"That son of a bitch just looked back at me!" The guy wasn't trying to be funny, either. The guy was a good player, but he had the shakes. All Jimmy could say was, "Ooohhh, where are the guys in the white jackets?"

⎯⎯⦿⎯⎯

Most golfers consider it an honor backed by great tradition to be invited to play in the Masters, which is the first of the four major tournaments played each year as a rite of sorts that officially kicks off spring, albeit the second week in April. Controversy continues to rage on, though, regarding the pecking order of the four majors in terms of strength of field and significance of an event that typically has fields of fewer than a hundred golfers, with numerous golfers falling through the tournament's strict qualifying criteria. Then there's the course itself—beautiful and almost impeccably groomed every year, yet supposedly set up to favor long, high-ball hitters who can draw the ball right to left. The golfer probably best known for never being a good fit at Augusta is Lee Trevino, who has six major titles to his record— two apiece in each of the other three majors. Veteran PGA Tour golfer Ken Green offers up his own assessment of the Masters' standing in the great scheme of things:

Somehow over the years the Masters has become one of those majors that you're just "supposed" to play. Golfers get pressured to play majors even when they don't really want to. Maybe it's because they just don't feel the course suits their game or whatever. That could be the case with Lee (Trevino), yet he's taken some criticism for not playing Augusta a few times when he was eligible. It's kind of like the beating Scott Hoch took from other players one year when he skipped the British

Open. If he didn't want to go, that was his deal, no one else's. In that respect. I don't think people have given Lee the benefit of the doubt. If he doesn't feel Augusta suits his game, and he's never really played that well there, then it was certainly okay for him in his own mind when he didn't play there. It's like on the regular tour: You might play some event ten times and never do squat there, then decide never to go back. Why should it be any different just because a tournament happens to be called a major? It's a weird deal.

Jack Nicklaus has long been a friendly rival of Trevino's, starting about the time Trevino was first making a household name of himself by winning the 1968 U.S. Open. Trevino has never really been in contention on Sunday's back nine at the Masters, even though he once led after thirty-six holes back in the 1980s—when he was well into his forties. Trevino's game has always been one of hitting low fades, which works against him on an Augusta layout that favors the right-hander who can draw the ball. Stories also have persisted over the years that Trevino was simply uncomfortable at Augusta, a private and secretive club that always has been overwhelmingly waspy, and he would often avoid going into the clubhouse or locker room, instead choosing to change his shoes in his car out in the parking lot. Trevino declined to play at Augusta a couple of times early in the 1970s, only for Nicklaus to intervene and help nudge Trevino back to Augusta. Nicklaus elaborates:

I would like to think I had a small hand in Lee Trevino's decision to play in the Masters in 1972 after (his) passing up the tournament the previous two years. I had developed great respect for Lee Buck Trevino as I got to know him better following his 1968 U.S. Open win, and somewhere along the line—probably when we teamed together to win the World Cup in November of 1971—I told him I thought it a shame that a player of his caliber did not give himself a chance to win all of the major championships. Lee responded that his game simply wasn't suited to the Augusta National course, first, because he wasn't long enough, and second, because the course was built for right-to-left shots and he was a left-to-right player. I told him that was baloney. "Lee," I said, "your game is good enough to win anywhere you believe you can win, and if it's good enough to win the U.S. and Canadian and British Opens back-to-back, then it's certainly good enough to win the Masters." Trevino never came close to winning at Augusta, but I am glad he played in the Masters a number of times after we talked. His record and his personality were such that his absence took something away from any great golf tournament.[11]

Part of the mystique of the Masters and Augusta National is in the almost tragic way that good and even great golfers have lost the tournament, beyond something as comparatively routine as an opponent's well-timed birdie putt or a splashed tee shot at sixteen. No Masters moment is more memorable for longtime viewers of the tournament than what transpired at the end of the 1968 Masters, when Roberto de Vicenzo signed a scorecard with an incorrect score, giving him one more stroke than he actually took and thus knocking him out of what should have been a playoff with Bob Goalby. The scoring snafu occurred at the seventeenth hole, where de Vicenzo had actually made a

Beginning in the late 1960s, Jack Nicklaus and Lee Trevino took their turns in golf's spotlight by winning majors galore. Nicklaus, however, was the only one of the two to ever figure out Augusta, winning six green jackets to none for Trevino. (Library of Congress)

birdie three, only for playing partner Tommy Aaron to write down a four. When de Vicenzo checked his scorecard after his round, he failed to notice the additional stroke at seventeen and he signed the scorecard. Sportswriter **Dave Kindred** was sitting in the press bleachers at eighteen that day when he turned around and saw de Vicenzo seated glumly at a chair by the scoring tent, having just learned the awful truth. Ironically, de

Vicenzo, a British Open winner, never won a major played on American soil, while Aaron went on to win the Masters five years later:

I remember I was sitting there with Ron Coffman of *Golf World*, watching the finish. I'm not sure how far ahead of the last group de Vicenzo had finished, but I know it was some time ahead. Coffman and I looked over at the scoring tent, which actually was just one of those patio umbrellas between the putting green and the clubhouse, and we noticed that de Vicenzo was just sitting there and that he looked forlorn. I can remember seeing him leaning over with his head in his hands.

We had no idea what had happened, but we soon discovered what had. I can remember chasing Tommy Aaron to his car in the parking lot to get Aaron's side of what happened. That's about all I remember of that, and I don't really remember what Aaron said. The one great quote came from de Vicenzo, when he said, "What a stupid I am." I didn't hear him say it, but I've read it so many times it's almost as if I heard him say it. In writing my story that day, I wasn't one of those guys who called for the rules to be changed. I thought de Vicenzo had made a mistake. But he owned up to the mistake like a man, was gracious about it, found no fault with Aaron, and found no fault with the Rules of Golf. It was one of those instances where the Rules of Golf are so honorable, that even in that most disheartening of circumstances affected by what obviously is an odd rule, he wouldn't complain about it. You would hope that a mistake like that could be rectified, but people hold the Rules of Golf almost sacrosanct.

A lot of people were blaming Tommy Aaron, that it was all Tommy Aaron's fault. But it's not Tommy Aaron's fault: It wasn't then and it isn't now. Aaron made a mistake, but ultimately the player is responsible for his own card. The player has to know what he made and then check each hole, making a mark beside each one. It was up to de Vicenzo to make it right, and I don't think he ever blamed Aaron, either. The two primary focuses among most media people that day were that it was Aaron's fault and that the rule was bad.

Herbert Warren Wind, a golf writer of a generation older than Kindred's, checked in soon after the de Vicenzo blunder with this account:

I don't think there is much to be gained from discussing the way the error was discovered, or de Vicenzo's sportsmanship in his hour of misfortune, or Goalby's graciousness. (De Vicenzo, despite his halting English, made a thumping good speech at the presentation ceremony, in which he blamed the scorecard error entirely on himself and went as far as to say that the pressure that Goalby had put on him perhaps accounted for his making the error. Goalby was direct and unmistakably genuine in declaring his sympathy for de Vicenzo, an old friend, and in stating that he would have much preferred to win the Masters in a playoff.) What had been a glorious day of golf and the climax of an extraordinarily exciting tournament had been turned to ashes by an arithmetical technicality. I know that the moment I heard the official announcement I was struck numb. All of a sudden, it was "Alice in Wonderland" time. The minute before we had been talking apples, and now we weren't even talking grapes—we were talking one-horse shays.[12]

———

As of 1999, Masters tickets still were an amazingly good bargain at a hundred dollars a pop. The price hadn't gone up in years. As affordable as a Masters ticket is, however, it is all that much harder to even get the chance to pay face value for a ticket. The waiting list for tickets had been closed for many years as longtime patrons typically will them down through their families. **Sam Snead** *has seen the ticket scalpers while driving into Augusta National every year, and he knows the lengths people will go to to get their hands on the precious but few tickets:*

A ticket to the Masters is the hardest ticket in sports, although they could handle more people down there. But what's good about the way it is now is that spectators can see two or three holes from one spot, such as at Amen Corner. I can remember one time riding from the course out to the house I was renting and being stuck in slow traffic. We could see a guy off to the side of the road with a sign that said, "Need Tickets." I rolled down the window and told him, "You're not by yourself. There's a lot of people without tickets." That's when he told me they were going for two thousand dollars apiece (closer to ten thousand dollars now, several years after Snead said this). That's incredible. They (actually) sell for a hundred dollars apiece. A Masters ticket is one of those things where people say, "I've got to have it." It's like wanting to eat something that to you is the best thing in the world to eat—you've just got to have it and are willing to pay about anything to get it.

The Masters and Augusta weren't always this popular. Three factors helped it get there, and their names were Hogan, Palmer, and CBS. **Frank Chirkinian,** *former CBS-TV executive producer of golf, adds some perspective to the evolution of the Masters' mystique quotient:*

Back when I started working the Masters telecast (in 1959), the tournament didn't have quite the attention it has now because golf was a relatively unknown thing as far as television is concerned. Arnold Palmer had just emerged as a potential superstar and the Snead-Hogan era was winding down. It didn't have the universal appeal because Europeans and the Japanese didn't see the telecast in those days. Today, the Masters goes into more than one hundred countries. It's akin to people tuning in to see the Kentucky Derby—that's the one horse race most of them will watch all year. Part of the tournament's appeal is that it's conducted at the same venue year after year. People are very comfortable with Augusta. They can turn it on at any moment and see the action at, say, the fourteenth hole and know immediately that they are seeing the fourteenth hole.

---

*The elements that make Augusta National and the Masters Tournament so special are in part man-made and in part circumstantial. Veteran golf writer **Al Barkow** is familiar with both types of influences:*

I think of the Masters in moments, and I think of when Norman blew that big lead (in 1996). I had never seen anything like that in a major championship or any kind of tournament for that matter. One of the nicest things I remember about it was when Nick Faldo gave Norman a big hug on the eighteenth green when it was all over. That was one of the nicest sportsmanship things I've ever seen because the guy had suffered, and Faldo just sort of gave him a hug. For Faldo that was pretty unusual—a gesture of warmth.

Then there's Nicklaus in 1998, when (at age fifty-eight) he got close to the lead. This was when he was obviously hurting with a bad hip, yet he had the stuff to rise up and get into position. He birdied number two and then came to three and chipped into the hole, and I almost had tears in my eyes. Here's this old guy, one of the greatest players of all time—I was in the middle of the crowd and the roar was just deafening. You get a little more sense of that kind of stuff happening there because of the nature of the place, with all the trees. You don't get that at the Open. But I like the British and U.S. Opens a lot better because I think they are true championships.

The idea of calling the Masters winner the tournament winner instead of tournament champion is all part of the clever way they do things. Clifford Roberts was one of the shrewdest promoters there ever was—he made something out of that place, which makes him some kind of genius. All this understatement, and no mention of money, and money is a big issue there all the time and it's getting even bigger. They're making millions in that tent where they sell all the stuff now. It used to be the only place you could buy shirts and all those other souvenirs was in the pro shop. There was an incredible jam in there. Japanese guys would go in there and just clean out the shelves. They didn't even look at the size or anything; they would just pay for it in cash and put it in the trunks of their Cadillacs parked right in back there on the driveway by the pro shop. It was incredible. People at the Masters finally said, "Whoa," and they opened up this enormous tent as a store, and it is just incredible. No one knows for sure because they won't tell you, but people who know that business estimate they must do $4 to $5 million of business that week. So they're very much into money, but very clever how they make it seem so genteel and understated.

⤞⫘⫘⤝

Larry Mize *grew up in Augusta, and while he never played the entire Augusta National course until he competed in the Masters for the first time in 1984, his local roots should have better prepared him for dealing with the nerves of playing in the Masters—at least you would think:*

I first played in the Masters in 1984, earning a spot in the field by winning in Memphis the previous year for my first victory on the PGA Tour. I showed up on that Monday in 1984 to play my first practice round and remember it as being cold, and it might even have been raining. So all I did was tee off and play down the tenth, and then come back up the eighteenth. It was so tough that day that I was hitting a three-wood into the eighteenth green for my second shot.

I came back out the next day and started out on number one. This time, I was so nervous that my hands were shaking, and I had a hard time keeping the ball on the tee. I finally was able to swing, only to duck-hook my ball into the trees on the left. When I got over there and saw where I was, and because this was only a practice round, I was getting ready to toss my ball back into the fairway. But there were spectators there telling me, "No, no, you've got to play that shot." So I did. The same thing happened to me on Wednesday. I again duck-hooked it left into the trees and had to play it from there. So by the time Thursday rolled around for the first round of the tournament, I wasn't quite as nervous on the first tee. I had gotten most of it out of my system with those two duck-hooks. This time, I ripped it down the middle, and I was so glad. It had been so nerve-wracking. As it turned out, I finished eleventh in my first Masters, and that was exciting because it meant I was automatically in for 1985.

---

*In the 1960s and early 1970s, **Doug Sanders** deserved the dubious title of best golfer never to have won a major, although he came very close a number of times, including one instance at the British Open when he missed a gimme putt. Sanders's best shot at winning at Augusta came in 1966, and while he still*

didn't win it that year, he never lost sight of where he was play-
ing and what his surroundings were:

If I had birdied the sixteenth hole on the weekend in 1966, I would have won the Masters. But I knocked it in the water and made five. I lost it by two strokes. Henry Longhurst was in the back of the green, and when I knocked the ball in the water, he says, "'Doug' Sanders has gone to his watery grave." I don't think I have ever liked water since—I don't think I drank water for ten years. Of course, now I don't drink anything but water. It's been six years since I've had a drink. I've found Christ and I've changed my life around.

Augusta National to me is the class and style, in any way you could possibly think about. To walk along and just see the magnolias and smell all the flowers—that's wonderful. Spectators can only see one side of the fairway at a time, but when you're walking down the middle of the fairway you can look over on both sides and see everything. And then you get up on those greens and people can't really tell just how fast they are because they're not up there. Sometimes you can drop a coin and it might slide three feet before it stops. But it's one of the prettiest places in the world. When going around the eleventh, twelfth, and thirteenth holes—Amen Corner—and then later going to the sixteenth: Your blood is just pumping.

It's hard to play there sometimes because you're look-ing around so much to see what else is going on, and you're looking at the scoreboard. You see guys go from being in the lead to tenth in three holes—bang, bang, bang. Some guy puts it in the water at thirteen and fifteen, and some other guy makes birdie, eagle, and you end up with a five- or six-shot swing in a space of just three holes. It is another place. Just to go there and smell the flowers and look around. There's no place like it. It truly is one of the greatest places that God has ever given to any golfer or anyone who has ever seen such beauty. Everyone there has always been gentlemanly and classy to me, and you just don't see that that much.

―――

*Being from Georgia, **Sanders** had long held on to a dream to play at Augusta National, which certainly was a lofty goal for a farm kid born to parents who didn't know or care about the game:*

When I was a boy, my dad said, "Son, when in the hell are you ever going to grow up to be something? You could go work at the service station and make fifty cents an hour. You could probably get a job, but you're out on the golf course and that will never amount to anything. Give me that club and I'll show you how to hit it." So I teed it up for him and he took a two-handed grip, hit it about sixty or seventy yards through the air, and said, "See, I told you it wasn't that hard to hit that ball."

We were from Cedar Town, Georgia. We lived up there on the farm, and until I was eight years old I thought my name was Gettinwood. Later I would bring my parents down to watch me (at the Masters). They would be sitting up there in the stands where I could see them. Hogan and all of those guys would drop their clubs down after hitting some balls on the practice tee, and I could see my dad sitting there saying, "Hell, if they want me to go down there and show them how to hit that ball, then I'll go down there and show them."

I first went down there when I was seventeen to play in a national junior qualifier at Augusta Country Club. While I was down there, we rode by Augusta National, and I said, "Man, oh man, someday I want to go on there and play. I'm going to work hard." And I did, and I've got a great picture of Palmer, Nicklaus, and me walking off a tee there.

I played with Nicklaus during his last Masters round as an amateur. I've stayed there in the cottages and gone

Augusta's par-three sixteenth hole provides one of the dozens of pristine settings that comprise part of the mystique here. On this occasion, Tiger Woods, Jose Maria Olazabal, and Seve Ballesteros are together for a practice round prior to the 1997 Masters won by Woods in record fashion. (AP/Wide World Photos)

back there to play golf with some buddies. It's got some style and class to it that you just don't find anymore. Most all of the other golf clubs now are subdivisions. They've got houses everywhere. Thank goodness, we've still got a few of the places like Pine Valley that built golf courses—built to play golf. Cypress Point, too. Places like that weren't built because of all the money you can make by building and selling homes. You don't find that today. Some of those new development courses are like ten thousand yards long when you include the distance from the clubhouse to the first tee and then the distance between each of the eighteen holes, going from one green to the next tee. Give me Augusta any day.

———

*Another aspect of the Augusta National and Masters tradition is in how one conducts himself or herself, as in the case of running on the grounds. As golf writer **Melanie Hauser** found out one day, that is verboten.*

I got called down for running. I've even seen players get called down for running. I mean, you're kind of running along and a security guard just looks at you and says, "We . . . don't run . . . at Augusta." I was running from the clubhouse out to the locker room area and the player was running from there to the parking lot area.

(Golfer) Billy Andrade once accidentally walked into the champions locker room before they put the big door on it. It used to be a swinging door like a saloon-style door. I remember Billy telling me the story of walking into there and stealing something off of the buffet, and a little man gave him a hard time about it and he was like, "Yeah, right. Whatever," and he walked out and asked, "Who was that guy anyway?" It was Gene Sarazen.

Masters practice rounds are almost as popular as tournament rounds, although the crowds seen on Tuesday and Wednesday are distinctly different from the folks who show up on Thursday when the tournament itself starts. Early-week patrons are for the most part younger, able to get in because practice-day passes are much more accessible. Once Thursday rolls around and the festive atmosphere has given way to serious behavior, onlookers in attendance seem to be a bit older and wiser, although no less enthusiastic. Author **John Feinstein,** *in his 1999 book* The Majors, *offers a glimpse into crowd makeup at Augusta:*

The Thursday crowd is very different from the practice-day crowds. It is older, to say the least. "It's a mature crowd," Justin Leonard said with a grin. The Masters is the toughest ticket in sports. The last time there was a public sale was in 1972. The waiting list for those trying to get tickets was cut off in 1978. Each ticket is red-bordered with a picture of the clubhouse in the middle and the $100 price for the week at the bottom. It also has a number that allows the club to track it if it is lost or turns up in the wrong hands. If someone misbehaves on the grounds, his ticket is removed, the number traced back to the owner, and that person is removed from next year's ticket list. No one misbehaves at Augusta.[13]

---

*Veteran television and radio sports journalist **John Derr,** still spry and active in his eighties, has seen Augusta and the Masters add a new dimension to its allure with its worldwide broadcasts:*

After I did the television in this country I did the overseas telecast for the club, and it went to 133 countries. I did that for about four or five years. We had 660 million viewers, if you can imagine making a mistake and having 660 million people seeing your mistakes.

In this regard, I had a funny experience with Jose Maria Olazabal the (first) year he won (in 1993). I saw him Sunday night coming down from the clubhouse to the press room, and he saw me and he called to me, "John, my grandmother heard you today." At that time Jose spoke rather poor English, and I said, "Where's your grandmother, Jose?" And he said, "Home."

"Oh, home here or home in Spain?"

"Home in Spain."

"That's good; I'm glad she saw you. Did it go into Spain in English or translated into Spanish?" I asked this because we had six countries that translated and all the rest of them took English. When I asked, he said it came in English.

I said, "Oh, good, Grandma understands English!"

"No, no, she no understand English, but she understand eagle at fifteen!"

———

Yet another part of Augusta National's mystique is as a rich, private, and gorgeous club situated on the outskirts of a mid-sized southern city that is mostly middle class and below. Two

worlds have collided and each has its own particular charm.
Curt Sampson, *author of* The Masters, *saw things in researching his book that conjured up familiar memories from his own past:*

I'm a golf fan, so I want to know what golf club Nicklaus, say, hit to fifteen in '73, but that stuff, while interesting and vital, is covered by *Sports Illustrated* and your daily newspaper. I was most interested to find out some of the interaction between the town and the club and the tournament, and that interaction turns out to be mostly via some of the poorest people in Augusta, such as the caddies—historically, although now the caddies are white and, I think, middle class, and there's money in it. But in the old days, Augusta interacted with Augusta National via caddies and other club employees. That's just the kind of collision I've always been interested in. Since I was a caddie at an expensive Jewish club and most of us caddies were poor, and most of us were black, that kind of thing is very interesting to me—the disparity between income levels and education.

Dave Kindred, *sportswriter, likewise sees the dichotomy between Augusta National and Augusta, the city:*

It's a different world. You go outside the gates and you're in Augusta, and Fort Gordon is right next door and the downtown is like an army town. It's much better than it used to be, however, because in the fifties and sixties there wasn't much there. The club is there, but it's not really part of the city. You go there and find that the club isn't really part of the world, either. That's part of the attraction of it; part of the guilty pleasure of it. That's why Lee Trevino chose to change his shoes in the back end of his car. He didn't want to be a part of this world that Augusta maintains. He always made a big deal out of how he couldn't play Augusta. He had a chance to win one of his early times there, but shot something like 80 on Sunday. He could play there. He could play anywhere. He could hit every shot; he could get it up and down from anywhere. I don't think he liked that atmosphere, and I can understand that. I can remember the first time Calvin Peete (an African-American golfer) played there, maybe the only time, I'm not sure. Some of us were asking if he enjoyed playing there, and he said, "That's like asking my grandfather if he enjoyed slavery." But he played. He came down Magnolia Lane, he said, in a limousine driven by a friend because he had always said if he played there he would be taken down Magnolia Lane in a limo.

THE MASTERS

There were all these "millions" of people pulling for Palmer, and there I was, this little guy from South Africa, and only my wife and my dog were pulling for me.

—GARY PLAYER

The Masters Tournament is the first of the four majors played every year, and it marks the beginning of spring on most golfers' calendars. But while first on the list, is it the best of the four majors? Let the arguments begin. It certainly is the most anticipated each year, and its uniqueness among the four as being the only one played on the same golf course year after year has bred a world-wide familiarity that equates to being the best. Many golfers, however, take a different tack. They say that the Masters' invitational criteria and resultant small fields drop it down to somewhere in the middle of the list of majors, with good golfers occasionally falling through the cracks in the invitational criteria.

But does it matter if the Masters doesn't come out on top of computerized studies or golf's version of the Sagarin Ratings? Probably not. The point is to take it as it is—an annual source of golfing excitement that brings golf's past, present, and future together in a setting that is ideal and set up for great, wonderful golf shots, where risk and reward are around every corner, and where Jack Nicklaus can make one more go of trying for yet another green jacket.

The Masters is what it is because of the masters who have brought their A games—and sometimes less—there to compete in the spirit of one of the greatest golf competitors of them all, Bobby Jones. Gene Sarazen won numerous other major tournaments, but none as memorable as the double-eagle win he posted at Augusta in 1935. Ben Hogan won twice as many U.S. Opens as he did Masters Tournaments, but it is a Masters that Hogan didn't win that forever established his vital link to this southern golf mecca—referring to the third-round 66 he shot four months shy of his fifty-fifth birthday in 1967, practically crawling his way up the eighteenth fairway on legs much older than the man. Then there's four-time winner Arnold Palmer, who in the late fifties and early sixties partnered with CBS-TV to bring Augusta and television golf coverage into the forefront of the American sporting scene. Then came Nicklaus, and Gary Player, and Watson, Seve Ballesteros, Faldo, and Tiger. And that doesn't even count the masters who haven't won at Augusta, even though they're inexorably linked to the place—masters such as Norman and Roberto De Vicenzo, and even Bobby Jones himself.

The Masters might not be the best of golf's four majors, but it has always been the brightest.

An invitation to play in the Masters Tournament remains a cherished goal for golfers, and a victory at Augusta is rewarded with a lifetime exemption into the event. Then it's up to the green jacket winner to decide when enough is enough and to quit playing there when his game no longer cuts it. Still, that unspoken rule hasn't prevented some past champions from overstaying their welcome in the field—Doug Ford perhaps being the most notorious example. **Sam Snead** *offers some insight on getting into the Masters and what it takes to stay there:*

Not all of the best players get into the Masters each year. Yet it's the easiest one to stay in (in terms of qualifying for the next year's tournament) unless you're playing something close to bogey golf. If you win it, you get a lifetime exemption. Still, I remember (Clifford) Roberts once telling everyone at the dinner that if any of us ever felt we weren't competitive anymore, that it would be up to us to decide when it was time not to play the Masters anymore. He said, "When you don't feel competitive anymore, just come to the dinner and plan to play in the par-three tournament (on Wednesday)." It's the top tournament in the world. I think eight out of ten golfers would rather play Augusta than any other tournament in the world.

⸺∞⸺

A long-standing tradition of the Masters has been its open-arms policy toward accepting amateurs into its field, obviously a throwback to the ideals emulated by the greatest amateur golfer of them all, Augusta National cofounder Bobby Jones. The Masters' qualifying criteria have been modified over the last few

*decades to cut down on the number of amateurs in the field,
such as no longer giving the entire Walker Cup team free entry
into the tournament. Had it not been for that qualifying clause
in the past, **Billy Joe Patton** never would have had the chance
to contend for the Masters title in 1954. In what perhaps was
the most memorable amateur showing in Masters history, Patton
led the Masters on the weekend, and despite a stumble on
Saturday that left him five shots out of the lead, he recovered on
Sunday and had climbed back to within a shot of the lead by
tournament's end. Patton, a retired lumber salesman now split-
ting time between his native North Carolina and Florida,
recalls:*

The first time I ever played in the tournament was in
1954, although I had played the course once about four
or five years before that. I was surprised that I was able to
play as well as I did. At least, I didn't have the type of
record that suggested I should be within a stroke of
golfers like Sam Snead and Ben Hogan in the Masters
Tournament.

I got an invitation to the Masters in early January
that year. Betsy, my wife, had just given birth earlier that
month to what turned out to be our last child, and I
knew we wouldn't be able to go to Florida for me to practice for the tournament. But I felt like I would never
again be invited, so I tried to hit as many balls as I could
at home during lunch breaks. Then we'd close the office
by 4:30 and by the end of January I was hitting the ball a
little bit better. By the end of February I was hitting the
ball quite a bit better, well enough so that I went down
to a local tailor shop and had them make me a white
jacket. Betsy asked me, "Sweetie, why did you have them
make you a jacket?" and I told her, "Well, I'll need some-

thing nice for the presentation." I had hit so many balls that I was feeling real good about my game. Actually, though, I hit those many balls to avoid embarrassing myself. It just turned out nice. I probably was much better off by not winning the tournament. People get a lot of sympathy when they finish close without winning. More than that, it would have been difficult for me to handle the money, the whiskey would have been a problem, and with the women I would not have had a chance. (Patton is joking.)

The invitation came in the mail from the club. It was from Bob Jones. He was eager to have amateurs playing in the Masters Tournament in those days and he wanted to get as many there as he could, so they not only invited the Walker Cup team, they invited the alternates as well, and I was an alternate.

They were also trying to sell tickets, and early in the week of the Masters they had a driving contest. I went down to hit my balls and I hit the first one pretty solid, and they called back "3-3-8." I think that won the contest by eight or nine yards, and that raised my confidence even more. Besides, I knew I was a good putter and I thought if I hit the ball farther off the tee than the other players, then maybe I should be there.

I shot 70 the first round and 74 the second, and I was tied for the lead. I think I shot 75 in the third round. My mother and father had gone down for the tournament, but they left Sunday morning and drove back home to Morgantown (North Carolina), the reason being, my father said, that I wasn't playing my game when I shot the 75. So I started the fourth round five strokes in back of Ben Hogan. I then made the hole in one at six and

North Carolina amateur Billy Joe Patton surprised the world and perhaps even himself when, in 1954, he grabbed the first-round lead at the Masters. Here he shows his scorecard to his admiring mom, N. M. Patton, outside the Augusta clubhouse. (AP/Wide World Photos)

birdied two, eight, and nine—all after a bogey at number one. I was out on the front side in 32, and think I caught Hogan by the tenth tee even though we weren't playing together. I remember standing on the tenth tee and looking at the scoreboard beside the eighteenth green, and I saw that Hogan and his gallery were coming up the seventh fairway. I could tell by his score that if he parred seven, eight, and nine, we would (in essence) be tied with nine holes to go, and I felt real fortunate, thinking back to the time when I had sat on a little boat rocking around in the Pacific Ocean during the Second World

War, glaring out at the ocean water and wondering if I would ever get an opportunity to play in a big tournament to find out how good I was. So I felt real lucky to be standing on the tenth tee at Augusta that day with nine holes to go and tied for the lead.

I played as well as I could on the back nine, but I had a bad hole at thirteen and made a seven. My second shot there was a four-wood into the green, and if it had been a step—three or four feet—to the left, I would have had a ten- to twelve-foot putt for an eagle three. A lot of people have written or made comments about what a terrible shot I hit, but if the ball had been just a small step to the left I would have had a reasonable putt for an eagle three. Where I think I really lost the tournament was at the fifteenth, because I came back to birdie the fourteenth hole—driver, eight-iron to within six inches of the cup. At the fifteenth I hit a hook so far to the left that my ball was lying on bare ground, and now I was faced with a tough second shot to the narrow green. I elected to go for the green, hitting a two-wood off that bare-ground lie. Actually, with that lie and by my using a two-wood, I couldn't have put the ball on the green one time in fifty. It was a stupid golf shot on my part. It wasn't a question of nerves; it was a question of judgment. Looking back on it, I should have laid up. But after making the seven at thirteen, I thought I had to have birdies, particularly at the fifteenth. Hogan was about forty to forty-five minutes behind me on the course, and he ended up making a five at thirteen and a five at fourteen, and I had played them in seven-three, so I hadn't actually lost any ground there. But I didn't know that—and I didn't believe you could make a seven at thirteen and not lose ground. I ended up missing the green at fifteen and took a seven there and ended up a stroke behind Hogan and Sam Snead, with Snead winning the playoff.

Playing as well as I did changed my life. People now knew who I was. The biggest change came just a few days after the tournament when I was invited back to Augusta to play golf with President Eisenhower, and all those pictures were taken of us playing together. Playing golf with the president and getting all that publicity meant as much to me as how I did in the tournament. Ike was a man's man. A complete gentleman. He loved his golf, he loved his bridge game, and he loved his friends. I played with him quite a few times after that. We played a lot after I joined the club. I joined there in 1957, resigned my membership in 1970, and then got invited back in 1984.

I ended up playing in the Masters for thirteen straight years, starting in 1954. I ended up as low amateur in 1954 and again sometime in the late fifties and then tied for low amateur in the early sixties. I remember that I was paired with Arnold Palmer four different times while playing in the Masters, and he won the tournament in each of those years (1958, 1960, 1962, and 1964). I don't know if I would say that I was Arnie's lucky charm, but I know he would say so. A few years ago we were standing around talking at some social function when I said, "Palmer, do you realize I played with you at one time or another in each of the four Masters Tournaments that you won?" He said, "Billy Joe, I was always more aware of that than you were."

I never turned pro because there really wasn't any

money in it in those days—not until TV came along. I knew I could make more money selling lumber to furniture manufacturers in North Carolina than I could out on the golf tour. I know that what I accomplished that year at Augusta certainly helped my sales career. In fact, golf helped my business immeasurably.

———

Through 1999 **Nick Price** *had never won the Masters, and his record there doesn't live up to the rest of his record in the majors, which includes two PGA Championship victories and a British Open triumph. But for one day in 1986, Price owned Augusta, shooting a third-round 63 that still stands as a tournament course record, tied by his good friend Greg Norman in the first round of the 1996 Masters. Price's memories of his 63 are Masters-crystal clear:*

The 63 put me one back of Greg Norman going into Sunday. I had shot 79 on Thursday, when I hit sixteen greens in regulation, only to have something like five three-putts and two-putts on every other hole. It was terrible, and I was so frustrated because it was my third Masters and still I had shown no sign of even playing the course well. I had missed the cut in both '84 and '85, and had prepared for my third Masters as well as I could, and then to shoot 79 in the first round. Things weren't looking good for me. The biggest problem I was having was putting—mainly the speed of the greens and the severity of the slopes. In general, when stimpmeter readings are taken of really quick greens, the reading will be around thirteen on the stimpmeter. But if you took a stimpmeter and ran it from the top left of the fourteenth green at Augusta, which is probably about thirty-five to forty yards wide, it would run right off the green. So there's a time when the stimpmeter probably doesn't even come into effect there because the green is probably about 140 on the stimpmeter. It's one thing to have greens that are relatively flat or don't have the severe slopes Augusta has, but when you combine that with the fast greens it makes things very difficult.

I had practiced hard and was hitting the ball really well going into Augusta in 1986. I don't know if I felt I had a chance to win, but I think the frustration of round one that year came out in rounds two and three. I had this resolve in me that I was going to make the cut and then get into the top twenty-four so that I would get exempt for the next year. Those were the two thoughts I had at the forefront in my mind when I went out for the second day.

I played really well and shot 69 on Friday, and I made the cut with a shot to spare. Things then went exceptionally well for me on Saturday. I now knew I could play the golf course after having played five over-par rounds in all my previous attempts. I don't think Augusta is suited for someone who hits the ball on a low trajectory, and that's a big part of my game. Even then, I felt if I hit the ball into the right positions and putted solidly, I could play the golf course. So I went out on Saturday with a whole new perspective on the golf course, only to hit my drive at one into the bunker and make a bogey there. No worry. I still had that new confidence in me, and I went on a birdie roll.

The amazing thing about the day is that I did not hit

any of the four par-fives in two. I laid up on every par-five. Obviously, my wedge game was in good order, and I putted phenomenally well. On the three holes I didn't birdie on the back nine—fourteen, seventeen, and

Nick Price went into 2000 still looking for his first Masters Tournament victory, but at least he still holds a share of the tournament course record. Here he is in the third round in 1986 at Augusta's eighteenth, closing out a record nine-under-par 63 that would be tied by his good buddy Greg Norman ten years later. (AP/Wide World Photos)

eighteen—I barely missed birdie putts. On fourteen I left my approach putt from twenty-two feet two inches short right in the mouth of the hole—one more roll and it would have gone in. On seventeen, I hit one of the best putts of the day, but just misread it, and it shaved the lip. At eighteen, after hitting a poor tee shot, I hit a four-iron up onto the green, about thirty feet away. From there I putted and my ball actually did more than a 360. It went in the hole and came out and actually crossed the line on which it had gone. It was a 450.

Thinking back to when I was in the middle of the back nine, I remember watching the other scores and thinking, *Hey, not only can I set the course record today, but if I keep playing like this I can win the tournament.* I was playing with Bruce Lietzke that day, and I remember him saying to me after we had finished—he shot 68: "This is the first time I've ever shot four under where it felt like two over." I was fired up. I felt I suddenly had the key to playing well at Augusta. After I had birdied thirteen it put me seven under for the day, and I knew I needed two more birdies to break the course record. I said to my caddie, David McNeilly, an Irishman who had caddied for Nick Faldo, walking up the fourteenth fairway, "Do you know what the course record is?" And he said no. I said, "It's 64." And he said, "Let's go." I didn't need any encouragement from him because I knew what position I was in, and I was also thinking that I could win this tournament. That's what was so exciting for me. I ended up with ten birdies and one bogey for the 63.

The two biggest holes for me that day were the birdies on fifteen and sixteen. I didn't feel like there was a lot of pressure one me, only that I had nothing to lose.

I hit a sand wedge on fifteen from about eighty-two yards and hit it about three feet behind the hole. I was left with a really difficult left-to-right downhill putt, extremely quick. But I knocked that one in. At sixteen, the par-three, the pin was cut in the middle of the green down on the bottom tier. If you hit it into the right spot on the right side of the green, the ball will feed on down to the hole. I turned a six-iron off the middle of the green, and I absolutely nailed it, just perfect. It pitched about two feet from the top of the downslope and fed down to about eighteen inches behind the hole. Again, I had another putt that I had to hit outside the hole. It was extremely fast and it went dead into the middle. All I had to do now was par the last two holes to set the record, but I wasn't thinking about pars, I was thinking about two more birdies. I always felt like when you get on a roll like that, the object is to post the lowest number that you can because the next day is going to be different, and sure enough the next day was a lot different for me. I didn't quite have the fire in my game. I think there was a bit of the nerves there, in the moment of playing in the last group of the Masters. More than anything else my putting let me down. If I had putted like I did the day before, I probably would have shot 67 or 68, which would have been good enough to win.

A lot of people expect when you play a really good round to go out and shoot another really good round the next day. I had shot three under the second day and I was playing much the same on Sunday that I had played on Friday, but I just didn't make the putts. I was a little tentative and that's what happens at Augusta when the pressure is on. If there is a weakness in your game, especially on the greens, you tend to get a little tentative and you don't quite hit the putts as positively as you should. I didn't have the authority on the greens.

The best compliment came from David Leadbetter, my teacher. After I shot 79 on Thursday, he was standing on the back of the eighteenth green, and after I had finished looking at my card I looked at him straight in the eye and said, "You know, I don't think I can play this course." And he said, "You can play any course you want to." Then on Saturday, when I walked off eighteen, he was again waiting behind there and he just had the biggest smile I've ever seen on his face and he said only, "You see."

I've never really struggled with the golf course, but I've never really felt all that comfortable, either. It doesn't really favor my type of game. That made that achievement all that much better for me. It's analogous to a high-ball hitter playing exceptionally well in the wind at the British Open. It just meant a lot to me that day, and I think the next best score that day was a 68, so the course wasn't playing all that easy.

Coming from the relative obscurity of shooting a 79 in the first round to a 63 on Saturday, it was like the whole Masters changed for me in four hours. At that stage in my career, I wasn't a winner. I had won one tournament over here (in the United States), which was the World Series of Golf, and I had probably won seven or eight around the world. I was still building my base, the foundation of my career. All of a sudden I was thrown into the deep end. It was unexpected. I spent an hour and a half or two hours in the press room talking about the 63, and then I had lunch and just didn't have as much time to practice because there was so much going on, but I thoroughly enjoyed every minute of it. There's nothing from that day I want to forget. My career has really been a buildup of successful little things at the beginning and then big things. Then when my game did explode, it really wasn't a surprise to anyone.

I had a hard time in the mid-eighties in that I was playing well, but I wasn't winning. I had played in the last group of a major championship four or five times and had been in contention in six or seven of them. That Sunday at Augusta I had a good opportunity to do something there, but I didn't take the bull by the horns. I was waiting for something to happen instead of going out there and making something happen with the right decisions. I'd trade the 63 in for a green jacket in a heartbeat.

―――――

Unlike Nick Price, Seve Ballesteros practically owned Augusta National and the Masters through the eighties. Ballesteros won the Masters in 1980 and 1983 and contended several other times, such as in 1986 when his approach shot into the water at fifteen drowned his chances of holding off hard-charging Jack Nicklaus and again in 1987 when he was eliminated from a playoff ultimately won by Larry Mize. By the end of the decade, however, Seve's game was starting to fade, although he still lived a charmed life of sorts at Augusta. That's what American golfer **Ken Green** *saw when paired with the Spaniard in the final round of the 1989 Masters:*

We were both something like three or four shots out of the lead, so we both had a chance. There had been a pretty bad rainstorm earlier, so the course was kind of muddy that day. The ground in between the second green and third tee, where spectators normally gathered, had turned into a sandbar. There were ripples of mud and heelprints where my ball ended up. I asked a nearby official for a drop because I had heard that the Masters had a crowd-damage clause allowing for a free drop, and this certainly was crowd damage. The guy comes over, takes a look at my ball, and says, "No, you have to play it as it lies." I said, "If this isn't crowd damage, what is?" But it didn't do any good, probably because of who I am.

Well, Seve shot something like a 31 on the front nine, only to hit a monster snipe (snap hook) off the tenth tee into the trees and into a soft drainage area. I look over and figure he's got no shot, that he's going to have to chip it back to the fairway. Then he calls for a ruling, and I can see he's getting ready to take a drop. That's when I walked back up the hill to where he was, and I said it wouldn't be legit to take a drop, that this was not crowd damage. But the rules official says it is crowd damage and tells Seve it's okay to take a drop. I said that wasn't acceptable, so I called for a second official. We were waiting for him to get there, when Seve said, "It's okay, Ken, you can leave. I'm not going to cheat." The other guy who came over was an R&A official. It took him just one second to look at Seve's lie and say that he would have to replace the ball where he found it, that there was no crowd damage there. My lie back between two and three had been much, much worse than Seve's, yet the initial rulings had gone opposite ways. But that's Augusta for you.

Later on in the round, we got to sixteen and it started pouring. The pin (of the par-three hole) was set back on the left—the usual Sunday placement. Seve hit a five-iron right at the pin, but it was a floater: There was no chance of it making it over the water. Seve stands there staring at his ball as it splashes into the pond. He just stands there and stares for something like forty-five seconds, trying to make it look like he's hit a great shot and is flabbergasted by the shot. Finally, he turns to me and says, "Can you believe this?" I said, "Yeah, get off the tee, it's my turn to hit."

Augusta's greens for Masters Tournament week might be the fastest in the world, and with all the undulations, it's not uncommon to see more than a few three-putts and even the occasional four-putt, as **John Feinstein** *points out in his book* The Majors:

Everyone has a story about the greens at Augusta. The most famous may involve two-time Masters champion Seve Ballesteros, who barely tapped a birdie putt on the sixteenth one day in 1986 and watched it roll twenty feet past the cup. He almost took a full swing at the next putt and was ten feet short. Then he missed the bogey putt for a four-putt five. Later, in the press room Ballesteros was asked what happened at the sixteenth. He shrugged and said in his Spanish accent, "I mees, I mees, I mees, I make." Then he stormed back to the champions locker room and began screaming at Tom Watson (as if he had any control) that the sixteenth green should be blown up.[14]

Oklahoma City oilman and amateur golfer **Charlie Coe** *first played in the Masters in 1949 and emerged as perhaps the best amateur ever to play in the tournament, a hair ahead of Billy Joe Patton on the unofficial list ranking great Augusta amateurs. Coe, an Augusta member, recalls his playing days from Masters past:*

The main idea was to have a good amateur field, and back in those early days they didn't distinguish between amateurs and professionals—everyone just played. My first time was in 1949. I've forgotten how I finished, it wasn't very high, but it was quite a thrill to play there. It was an awful lot of fun. We used to have a cookout, a pic-

Amateur Charlie Coe and Gary Player are all smiles following the 1961 Masters, won by Player. Coe was low amateur and tied for second that year with Arnold Palmer. (AP/Wide World Photos)

nic right there in front of the clubhouse. They'd put up a tent and we'd have some fried chicken, and just have a good time.

I knew Mr. Jones and Clifford Roberts very well. Both were very fine gentlemen. Mr. Roberts was a stickler for tradition and rules, and so was Bobby Jones. I was having dinner with Mr. Roberts once after I became a member, and I asked him what was the rule about something, and he said, "We don't have rules here, we just have customs." I've always lived by that statement. You can do whatever you want down there, except if you break a custom you're in deep trouble.

In 1961 I came in second, tied with Arnold Palmer behind winner Gary Player. I was playing very well at that time. I remember coming to the last hole on Sunday and I needed a birdie to tie Player, but I missed my putt and he won the tournament. Palmer hit a poor second shot into the right-hand bunker, then pitched it over the green and took three to get down, giving him a six as we tied for runner-up. I was playing with Palmer, and, of course, that was very exciting. You're really just paying attention to your own business and find out all of a sudden that you're right in the middle of things. Still, I didn't talk to him too much during the round.

People really got behind me at the end. A couple members of my family were there, too, and that added to the whole experience a little bit. I had a pretty good record down there, finishing fairly high in several of them. I liked the people, I like the golf course. I've known it well for many years and it's just a real fine golf course. My being on the Walker Cup team was what got me into the Masters in the first place, and I ended up playing in the tournament nineteen times. I eventually joined as a member in 1959. I never turned pro because my wife didn't want me to, and I didn't particularly want to, either. I was pleased and proud of the fact that I kept my amateur status all of these years. I'm sure Bobby Jones had some influence on me, but my wife and I sat down and talked about it and that was all there was to it. She said, "If you think I'm going to live out of a suitcase and raise a family, you're crazy."

I have an oil business and a few outside investments, but I'm retired. I've had a good life. I used to go to Augusta four or five times a year and now go about three times year. I got a chance to play golf with Eisenhower. He was a fun guy and a fair golfer. He had no feel in his hands. He was just as likely to hit a putt five feet as fifty feet.

I've been to fifty Masters Tournaments, covering every year since I first played there (in 1949). The course has really changed dramatically, and all for the betterment. The greens used to be harder than a rock with very little grass on them. And I've been through that transition and seen a lot of things change down there, and it's in perfect shape now. It's always fun to reminisce a little bit, but everybody has been awfully nice to me.

---

*In winning the 1961 Masters, South African **Gary Player** became the first non-American to win the Masters, although he probably wasn't the most popular winner as far as Augusta spectators were concerned. Player ended up edging Coe and Arnold Palmer by a single stroke, and this was after Palmer had* *double-bogeyed the seventy-second hole. Many observers of that Masters Tournament said that Palmer had blown the tournament, forgetting, however, that Player himself had actually had a four-shot lead at one time on the back nine. Player picks it up from there:*

There were all these "millions" of people pulling for Palmer, and there I was, this little guy from South Africa, and only my wife and my dog were pulling for me. It was understandable. I had a four-shot lead at one point, and still many people say that Arnold Palmer blew it on the seventy-second hole. *Sports Illustrated* was very kind, though. They said Gary Player won the Masters, pointing out that at the thirteenth hole I could have gone up the fourteenth fairway after I had hit my drive there into the trees on the right. But I couldn't move the people to make room for such a shot, whereas today I simply wouldn't play until they moved. So I just chipped it down onto the fairway, but knocked it down too far and it went into the creek, and I ended up with a seven. Then I got a (bogey) six at fifteen, and I still had to get it up and down on the last two holes to save pars. So I made seven and six on the two par-fives, but people forget that. I remember kissing my wife and getting the green jacket after I had won. It was a great thrill being the first non-American to win and a great thrill as well because of the admiration I had for Clifford Roberts, Bobby Jones, and President Eisenhower, and the disciplined way in which the tournament was run. It's a great place. The word that keeps coming back to me is *gratitude*.

*The greatest Masters master of them all had to be Jack
Nicklaus, whose six green jackets are two more than any other
individual golfer has won. At age fifty-eight in 1998, Nicklaus
again threatened on Sunday and, limping through the back nine
with a bad hip, still managed to finish sixth as Mark O'Meara
came from behind to win. Nothing, however, will ever take
away from the historic moment of Nicklaus at age forty-six in
1986 winning the Masters for a sixth time. Veteran sportswriter
Dave Kindred has been to the Masters about thirty times, but
the one that he missed was the big one that got away—the day
when the Olden Bear reinvented himself as the Golden Bear:*

Nicklaus in '86 was the only Masters I have missed since
1967. I couldn't be there because my son got married on
that Sunday. In fact, it was my birthday, April 12. I
walked into the house after the wedding and it was eight
o'clock at night. I turned on the television and the first
words I heard, a newsflash, said, "Jack Nicklaus today
shot 65," and I went, "Oh, (crap)." I told my son, "The
next time you get married, don't do it the second Sunday
in April," and when He did get married again he did it in
July. The 1975 Masters was another great one, with
Nicklaus, (Johnny) Miller, and (Tom) Weiskopf battling
it out. There are so many great memories. I can't tell you
how many times I've been in church listening to sermons
and instead I'm replaying Augusta rounds in my head.

——◦◦◦——

*Speaking of **Tom Weiskopf,** he checks in with a story that
brings some humor to what really was not a funny occasion. It
was sometime in the late 1970s at the Masters, and Weiskopf*

*was paired for his Sunday round with rival and former Ohio
State teammate Jack Nicklaus. It was one of those days when
Weiskopf could have made good use of a tee-side phone booth at
the first hole:*

Jack almost always wears green—green pants or something—on Sunday. This one time, he and I were paired
together for the last round of the Masters, fifth or sixth
from the last group. A phenomenal round would put
either one of us into contention.

Jack always warmed up on what I call the west side of
the practice range, and I always warmed up on the east
side. After I warmed up this time, I walked over to the
putting green about fifteen or twenty minutes before my
tee time. Then Jack walks over, and I can see we've got
identical outfits on: navy blue pants, white shirts, and
white shoes. I said to myself, *Now, how about this? Good
God, we've got basically the same look going for us.* Right
about then this big guy comes walking over to me, introduces himself, and says, "I'm from the FBI, Tom. I'm
going to be in the gallery today, and I need to tell you
this, that Jack has had a death threat. We don't think it's
anything serious, but we have to take it very seriously,
and you need to know this. I'm going to be walking very
close to you guys. Jack will have another guy and we'll
have people all through the gallery today. So don't get
too concerned."

Remember, this was at a time when Hubert Green
got his death threat while he was winning the U.S. Open
(in 1977), and there were some other ones that had happened earlier in the year. It was a period of time in which
you had to take this stuff seriously. I said, "Perfect." I

went over to my wife, Jeanne, and I said, "Jeanne, please go to the pro shop and buy me something like a powder-blue shirt." So she comes back and by now I'm on the first tee, where I take my shirt off and put on this powder-blue shirt. Everybody whistled and kind of *ooohhed* and *aaahhhed*. Jack came over and said, "What are you doing?" And I said, "Well, I just want to make sure that they don't shoot the wrong guy today." He chuckled. Neither one of us played worth a darn.

If a death threat couldn't shake Nicklaus, a Masters roar that came from somewhere else on the Augusta course could at times rattle him. Former Golf World *managing editor* **Ron Coffman** *recalls one such instance, which he believes took place in 1977, the first year Tom Watson won a green jacket, beating Nicklaus by two shots:*

I think that's the first time I ever saw Nicklaus choke. He was in the eighteenth fairway, getting ready to hit his second shot, when a roar went up at the seventeenth, where Watson had just birdied. And Nicklaus hit a terrible shot, really fat. I think maybe it was the only time I saw him distracted in going about his business.

Larry Mize, *the 1987 Masters winner, is unique among all the men who have won Masters green jackets. That's because Mize grew up in Augusta, although he was not a frequent visitor to the club, unless you include the many times he would play golf*

*at the adjoining Augusta Country Club and peek over the fence
at the Augusta National. Mize talks about growing up with the
world's best-known golf course practically in his backyard:*

My dad knew some members and played out there some,
but my dream was to wait until after I had qualified to get
into the Masters to play there. Actually, I did play it once
before I got into the Masters and that was around 1980,
although at the time they were changing the greens and
were using temporary greens. So while I played all eighteen holes, I didn't really play the whole course.

Most kids growing up and playing golf dream of playing in the U.S. Open, but for a kid in Augusta the
Masters is the dream. I first went out there to watch the
Masters when I was about nine or ten years old. I would
go out and get autographs and collect tees from players.
What I really loved to do was go to the practice range
and watch the guys hit, especially Jack Nicklaus and Tom
Weiskopf. Then in 1979 I remember having such a good
time watching Ed Sneed hitting balls that week (Sneed
and Tom Watson would eventually lose in a playoff to
Fuzzy Zoeller). Sneed was hitting it just so great. Even
when he was hitting fairway woods on the tee he was
knocking down his caddie (retrieving balls, common
practice in those days). It was incredible, and I later got
to know Ed.

You had to be a teenager to work there, like posting
numbers on the scoreboard, and I first worked there in
1972 and did it again in 1973. I was positioned at the
scoreboard at the third hole. In 1973, Sunday's round
ended up getting rained out and we had to come back out
on Monday, when Tommy Aaron came back to win it. I

can still see myself now, sitting there in the rain with a headset on listening for scores to be posted. What you could do at the scoreboard was poke your head through the holes and watch what was going on around you. I would work the morning shift and then get the afternoon off to go watch the play all over the golf course. There was still plenty of golf to see at that point. Even if you worked the afternoon shift, because you were only at the third hole you could leave after the last group went through, and there still was plenty of action left to see around the course.

⊸≈≈⊶

Scott Hoch entered the new millennium as one of the best PGA Tour players never to have won a major, and he's best remembered for the one that got away. That's what happened at Augusta in 1989, when Hoch missed a slick, downhill putt of two and a half feet that would have allowed him to beat Nick Faldo on the first hole of a sudden-death playoff. Instead, Hoch's miss left the door open for Faldo, who subsequently won the playoff with a twenty-five-foot birdie putt on number eleven for his first of what would turn out to be three Masters victories in an eight-year stretch. A week before Hoch returned to Augusta in 1990, he spoke to the author, then working for the Star-Telegram, *about time healing, in his case, still-fresh wounds:*

After this year's Masters, it (the missed putt) will be old news. There'll be no more worrying about it. Actually, I look back on last year's Masters as more of a positive experience than not. I was in the hunt until the very end, when others were dropping like flies. The public (though) has been very supportive and if nothing else, they know that Scott Hoch can play well and is a good golfer.

It has been more than twenty years since a first-time Masters contestant has won the tournament, that being Fuzzy Zoeller in 1979. It took **Mark O'Meara** *more than a dozen tries at Augusta before he finally broke through to win his first major in 1998, making a birdie at the seventy-second hole that gave him his first lead of that year's Masters. O'Meara once explained to the* Star-Telegram *why although Augusta appears tame to golfers playing a friendly or practice round there, it is a tough go for a golfer looking to drive down Magnolia Lane and win a Masters first time up:*

The odds are not in favor of the first-year player here. This course is one you need to play a lot in order to learn and understand it—to see how it changes depending on the weather conditions. There's also a lot of pressure. My first year here (1980), when I played as an amateur, I was paired with Fuzzy the first day and played awful, shooting an 80. In the practice rounds, I wasn't playing too badly. But then the tournament starts, and you're awed by the tremendous players. The greens speed up. Then it gets a little breezy. I thought I was in a whirlwind tunnel.

George Archer *was twenty-nine years old in 1969 when he won the Masters Tournament to earn his cherished green jacket. To get there, Archer earlier in the sixties had to go through an*

Augusta initiation of sorts by playing alongside golfing icon Ben Hogan. Hogan and Augusta are almost synonymous in golf lore, and Archer can be forgiven if he goes to his grave still associating the two institutions with one another:

The first time I met Ben Hogan officially, I was paired with him on Sunday in my first Masters. He had shot a very good back nine on Saturday and both of us were two off the lead, I think. The night before we played, I said to myself, *Well, when I'm an old man, I'm going to remember that I played with Ben Hogan and that's going to be something. So although I'm going to be too nervous to play well, I'm going to enjoy the day.*

I go out there the next day and can remember going up to him on the first hole and saying, "Mr. Hogan, George Archer." He just nodded his head, and I shook his hand. He teed off and hit a good drive, and then I went up there and drove it in the fairway. By this time, he was standing on the end of the tee up ahead. When I picked up my tee, I could see him standing there looking back at me and I was thinking, *Jeez, I didn't do anything wrong. I mean, I didn't move when he hit or anything like that, so what in the hell is he going to start chewing me out now for?* I mean, I was pretty intimidated.

So I got up next to him and he said, "George, that was very nice playing last week." I had won the week before in Greensboro, and now he starts talking, and we walk down the hill and he's talking, and he's talking and we walk to the bottom of the hill, and he's still talking, and we walk all the way up to the sand trap, and he's talking the whole time. My head is spinning around and I'm thinking, *What in the hell is going on here? The ice man,*

Ben Hogan holing another one at Augusta. (Library of Congress)

what is he doing? Oh! I get it: He's going to talk me to death, I see. All of a sudden I broke out laughing and he looked up at me and I said, "Excuse me, Mr. Hogan, I'm away," and I went over to my ball to hit. And I'm laughing because I was thinking, *Who the hell am I to think that Mr. Hogan is going to reverse-psychology me and talk me to death?*

Everything I had heard all my life—like he never says a word and you might get a "You're away" once in a while, and he never says, "Nice shot" or anything like that—that was not the Ben Hogan I played with. He was very cordial that day. We talked quite a few times while sitting on benches that day. The whole time I'm thinking, *Is this the Ben Hogan I've read and heard about?* He didn't play well—he hit about three bad shots, and he paid dearly for them. I got a two-stroke penalty and shot like a 78 and I think he shot a 75, and we both finished well back.

I played with him again the next year and with Arnold Palmer. That was an interesting day because twenty thousand people were out there watching Palmer and Hogan, and I was in the way. I'll never forget the third hole, where Palmer hit one of those low drives and the crowd roared like crazy. Hogan took the cigarette out of his mouth and threw it down on the ground. He threw it so hard, it bounced off my shoe. I was stunned. He then hit this little low fade and people clapped because it was down the middle. I then hit a three-wood down the left side. When we got down there, there was one ball about even with me and then the third ball about eighty yards ahead.

I got down there first to my ball. Meanwhile, Hogan and Palmer were walking and talking, and their caddies were with them, and all four walked right by the first ball near me, and they all went to the long ball up ahead. So I'm thinking, *Who's going to be the one to have to turn around and walk back to his?* Hogan got down there and never looked at the ball. He just puffed on his cigarette and looked at the green. Palmer had to bend over and look at the ball, and then turn around and walk back to his ball. And the crowd was like, "Wooooooooooo." Hogan sent a message there that was unreal, and that was, "There would be no more screaming for those Arnold Palmer drives." And there wasn't. He had a sand wedge to the green and the hole was about 400 yards long, so he had hit his drive about 310. Hogan was long when he wanted to be long. He could really rip it.

⚊⚊⚊

The most memorable and significant Masters Tournament victory of the 1990s was turned in by Tiger Woods, who won by twelve strokes in 1997 while setting a tournament scoring record with an eighteen-under 270. Woods, who's part African American, thus became the first black man to win at Augusta, twenty-two years after Lee Elder had broken the color line at the Masters. Elder was in attendance as Woods finished off his 1997 victory, as was golf writer **Melanie Hauser:**

To see the black waiters standing outside and to hear the caddies talking about what that moment meant to them, and to see Lee Elder walking out there, all that was so special. That night I called Charlie Sifford and got his take on it. This went beyond just a man winning a golf tournament. I think everybody will remember where they were and what they were thinking when Tiger Woods won the 1997 Masters. He wasn't playing just against men; he was playing against a number in the book and he was playing against history. For him to go out there and do that was fabulous—he was in a zone, and for it to be his first Masters as a professional made it even more special. It redefined so much about Augusta, and it tore down some walls. I thought back to the days when blacks were allowed only to be waiters and caddies at Augusta. It was an incredible moment. It wasn't as much a coronation as it was a redefinition of things.

The relationship between CBS-TV and Augusta's green jackets regarding coverage of the Masters Tournament has at times been tumultuous, even tense. Call it creative tension, though, with ideas generated over the years that have changed the face of television golf coverage for the better. In 1997, not long after he retired, former CBS-TV executive producer of golf **Frank Chirkinian** *talked about that relationship between network and private golf club, and spoke as if he were still part of the CBS team:*

CBS doesn't make any money off covering the Masters. We break even. What it does do is add prestige to the network in that it has become a corporate tapestry. To lose the rights to the Masters would be like losing one of our children, so it's important to do what is right to maintain that kind of relationship. It's a relationship CBS has learned to live with. It's just a question of getting together with them every year and going over what has been done in the past and what needs to be done for the future. The value in the relationship is more than just intangible. When we have that meeting each year, there's only one green coat there, and that's the chairman. It's always a cordial meeting. When Hord (Hardin) was the chairman, he'd always say, "Let's first play some golf, and then we'll sit down and talk." The meeting wasn't particularly long at first, but it has gotten progressively longer with additional international considerations. Every year it seems we were adding another vital organ: Japan, Germany, Spain, England, and on and on.

Today it's a metropolis, with offices and buildings put up to accommodate all the international feeds. There's more traffic in and out and so many more needs to think about. For example, we just can't interview when we want to because some of the international networks might not be prepared to handle an English-speaking player at a moment's notice (with CBS in the position of providing the video feed used by all). It's the club that represents all these international needs when we meet each year to discuss coverage. We didn't have this international problem when Cliff (Roberts) was there.

———⚹———

As far back as Chirkinian goes in the history of the CBS-Augusta marriage, broadcaster **John Derr** *goes back even further, back to the days before television invaded the Masters. Derr, now in his eighties, has seen about sixty Masters Tournaments, and he ranks Ben Hogan's 1953 victory as one of the most memorable. Hogan went on to win the Masters that year en route to becoming the first (and still the only) man to win three of the four modern-era majors in the same year:*

The most exciting day I ever saw Ben Hogan at Augusta was in the third round of the 1953 Masters. He was playing with Porky Oliver, and Porky was playing really well at that time. Porky shot 67 and Hogan shot 66, and I exhausted myself because I walked all eighteen holes with them. It was birdie here, birdie there, a flock of birdies, and they finished with a better-ball score of 31-29. And I think that was the most exciting round of the many, many, many rounds I ever saw at Augusta. Hogan termed it the best tournament of his career—he had opened with a 70 and then shot in the 60s the other three rounds.

In those days, this happened to be at a time when NBC had the rights to do the broadcast live. I had to go down to a studio in Augusta to do my post-tournament wrap-up. I was so exhausted that I couldn't finish. I kept drinking water and trying to talk, and people thought I was breaking up. It was just that I was emotionally spent as well as physically spent. But that was a great day.

I was able to walk around and see the course in those days of radio only, which as a TV guy you couldn't do. One time I was headed out toward Amen Corner and was going down the fourteenth fairway toward the tee. Horton (Smith) and his playing companion were coming up with their caddies, and Horton was just breaking up laughing, and I asked him what was so funny. He said, "I have just seen one of the funniest things I have ever seen out on a golf course." And he introduced me to Count Jean de Bendern, the English count he was playing with. Horton then said, "He put his ball into the creek at thirteen, and he went down and saw that he could play it because his ball was down on a little sandbar. So he sat down on a bank there and took his shoe and sock off and rolled up his pant leg, and he went down the bank to play his next shot. But he stepped off into the creek with the wrong foot. He had taken off his left shoe and sock, then stepped into the creek with his *right* leg and with the water up to his knee. So they're walking up the fairway and he says, "Come here and look at this," and sure enough his pant leg was wet all the way up to his knee.

—

*Credit **Derr,** too, with having a good case of foresight one year in the 1960s when it came time to pick a winner in a draw of players known as a Calcutta, a time-honored Masters tradition that eventually disappeared from public view when officially banned. In relating his story, Derr starts off by recounting the ceremonial first drive at the Masters:*

The thing that I will miss at Augusta is the ceremonial opening day with the old-time golfers. For years and years we had old Jock Hutchison and Freddie McLeod. And then for the last fifteen to twenty years, maybe longer, we had Sarazen and Snead and Byron Nelson. Of course, we lost Sarazen this year and almost lost Snead through one or more things, and Nelson has had a hip replaced and various other ailments. One of the distinctive features of the Masters is that early morning on Thursday, when the sun is coming up through the pine trees and the crowd gathers at the first tee and you see these great champions of yesteryear walk out there and still are able to hit it. Sarazen hit it this past year to the bottom of the hill, and Snead of course still hits it pretty well, part of the way up the hill.

I'm still fond of all those old-timers. You know, McLeod and Hutchison (unwittingly) helped make me a lot of money one day. We had a little Calcutta over at the *Sports Illustrated*–CBS party the night before the tournament started, and I had noticed that one of the players entered in the Masters was not on the list of entrants. Bob Drum was running the Calcutta and the secretary had typed up the list of the field, and there was one man whose name was not there. It was the same man who had told me that in his first twenty-seven holes of practice at Augusta, he had had thirteen birdies. And I thought, *God, he might be somebody I would want to buy a little ticket on.* But I didn't have much money.

The Calcutta went on for some time and eventually they auctioned off Palmer and Nicklaus and Player, and that was the end of the Calcutta. They were just about to close it down when I said, "Wait, wait, wait. Nobody had mentioned Jock Hutchison and Freddie McLeod, and I would like to make a bid of five dollars for Jock and Freddie." Well, a lot of guffaws went up from around the room, with comments about how they only played nine holes as ceremonial starters. I said, "That's all right. I'll buy Jock and McLeod and anybody else not bid on." Well, they knew that everybody had been bid off, but somebody says, "Aww, take his money," so I take the five dollars up and give it to CBS sports chief Bill MacPhail, and that closes the deal—I've got Hutchison, McLeod, and anybody else not bid off.

Well, the anybody-else-not-bid-off included the guy from Belleville, Illinois, later known also for being Jay Haas's uncle. I'm talking about Bob Goalby, of course. They had overlooked him in the Calcutta, so I bought him as a team with McLeod and Jock Hutchison and the payoff was $2,155, which I collected Sunday afternoon. My good friend Henry Longhurst, who was aware of my good fortune, wrote about me in the *London Sunday Times*, saying (Derr trills his *r*'s while imitating Longhurst's brogue), "This American correspondent who had had the foresight to bet on Bob Goalby for no apparent reason, had the further foresight to be paid off on a day when the pubs were closed."

Richard von Tacky, *a Titusville, Pennsylvania, golf club pro, got his ten minutes of fame in 1981, when he played in the Masters as an amateur. As von Tacky and hundreds of other amateurs from over the years can attest to, Masters week is* *much more than just two or four days of tournament golf. It is an unforgettable week-long experience:*

I was invited by virtue of being a semifinalist in the U.S. Amateur the previous year. I shot 76-85 at Augusta and missed the cut, even though I was playing pretty well. Unfortunately, I have the distinction of holding the undistinguished record for tying for the highest score ever recorded on number seven, the short straightaway par-four. It was the second day and I was one over with one three-putt. I hit my drive right into the middle of the fairway and had a sand wedge to the green. But then I hit it fat into a greenside bunker, and I made an eight. Two days earlier in a practice round I had holed it out from the same bunker for a birdie. It was kind of ironic. Still, the experience has lived with me forever. I could have played two years in row, but I turned pro in between. Still, people who introduce me today still refer to me as "the guy who played in the Masters." It's pretty neat.

To get there was unbelievable, a real accomplishment for me. I was twenty-three years old at the time. I arrived there the Friday morning of the previous week, played a practice round, and stayed in the Crow's Nest—I was the only one there. Same thing on Saturday. They had just refurbished the Crow's Nest. It was green and white, just beautiful: very cozy, very quaint, and a lot of fun to stay there. They just treat you like a king. Because it was my first time there and because I was an amateur, I felt like I was in the way. The longer I was there, though, the more I got used to it. At first you're thinking, *Is there anything I can be doing? Can I be doing the dishes or making the bed to make up for my being here?* It was pretty awe-inspiring.

Then my family and I rented a home in the suburbs of Augusta, like a lot of people do.

My mother and father, two sisters, my brother-in-law, and my wife and I stayed in a house. It was gorgeous, obviously. One sister isn't much of a golfer, but my older sister is so she understood. Still, my other sister was just excited to be there and she was very supportive. Basically, my whole family have been golfers for many years. Another thing about being at Augusta were all the phone calls that came to the house from people wishing me good luck. It was pretty neat.

I was lucky enough to be a member of Pinehurst Country Club through my parents. They had tour events there and I would see guys playing there. In fact, some would come in early and I would be at the range hitting balls and they would be hitting balls beside me. I played with big-name amateur people a lot, so I got a feel for it.

During a practice round on Sunday at Augusta, with virtually no one on the course, I caught up with Jack Nicklaus playing with three members, and I played through them on four. Jack just waved at me and smiled. I said hello and played through. I played practice rounds every day with Bob Tway, who was still an amateur then. We played with Hale Irwin one day, and Lon Hinkle and Andy Bean another. I knew Jay Sigel from all those years of amateur tournaments around Pennsylvania, and Jay and I played in the Par-Three Tournament together. As an amateur playing in front of sizable crowds, I had to get used to it. When you're playing well, it's no big deal, but when you're playing poorly you feel like everyone is watching you. I felt out of place when I got there, but less so as the week went on. It was especially tough hitting

balls on the practice range with caddies out there shag-
ging balls for you. It's not like you can hit a big cut and
everyone thinks you're working on your cut shot. If your
caddie is over here and you hit a big duck hook over
there, and he's got to go fifty yards to go get it, they know
if you're hitting the ball bad. That was a little weird.

The Par-Three Tournament was pretty nerve-
racking. I ended up one under and tied for fifth, I think,
and Bob was four under and tied for first. I don't know
what it's like now, but back then on the first three holes
you're hitting half-wedge, half-wedge, and, for me, an
easy nine-iron. It was like hitting down a bowling alley
with fifteen people deep on either side, and you're just
hoping you don't hit it on the hosel or blade it and kill
somebody. That's all I was thinking about.

When I shot the first-round 76, my short game was
pretty good, but I wasn't hitting the ball very well. I
bogeyed ten, eleven, and twelve after shooting one over
on the front—not all that bad for a kid from rural
Pennsylvania. The second day I was hitting the ball just
super. I parred one and was one under after three. I hit a
great shot at four, the long par-three down the hill, and
three-putted. At five I killed a drive and hit a five-iron to
eight feet and missed it. I bogeyed six—I had trouble
with six all week, but I was still feeling pretty good at just
one over. At seven, I piped it down the middle and had
a sand wedge to the green. But I hit it a little heavy and
put it in the bunker. I left it in there with my next shot,
left it in there again, then hit it about five feet above the
hole and three-putted from there for an eight. So now, I
go from feeling I can shoot 74 or 75 to thinking, Now
you've just made an eight. So there I was walking

through this crowd of people to the next tee and they're saying, "Don't worry about it, go get 'em," and I just felt like crying. I was so upset that I made double on eight and bogeyed nine. So I'm out in 44, then shot 41 on the back. I had the feeling like I had just survived a car accident. You know, you're not hurt, but your nerves are shot. I just couldn't concentrate. Even though you know you don't have a chance to win, you're trying to make the cut and it just goes on one hole. It was pretty devastating.

Regardless, just the fact that I played in the Masters and earned my way there is something that will always stay with me. I still have my badge and invitation as well as a book they send you after the Masters. I've got the scorecard and the yardage book in a trophy case with other stuff.

The number of foreign-born golfers invited into the Masters has long been a subject of contention from players around the world, and **Frank Beard** *is no exception. The Masters does offer a limited number of foreign exemptions at its own discretion, although the club recently modified its criteria to place more weight on the Sony world rankings:*

There used to be a kind of joke going around that while American-born professionals couldn't get into Augusta, a foreigner or someone of mixed race could get in. It was a sore point with many players. Chi Chi Rodriguez throughout the rest of the year was known (rightfully) as an American, but when it came to Masters week he was a Puerto Rican and he got in. You had guys from

Australia who had been living in the United States for years, such as Bruce Crampton, getting invited as foreigners. That rankled a lot of the rest of us. We knew in our heart that he was an American tour player. I'm not blaming him. But it was a bone of contention. At one time we players discussed the possibility of boycotting (the Masters) if nothing were done about (the makeup of) the field. We weren't really serious—it was just rhetoric. Still, some really good players weren't getting in: Every year there were about ten players better than half the field at Augusta who weren't playing there. There wasn't room.

I was one of those guys who, for whatever reason, almost always finished in the top twenty-four, which gave an automatic invite for the next year. That gives you an indication of the weakness of the field—I'm not talking about my game per se as much as I am the quality of the competition. I just seemed to win tournaments or finish in the top twenty-four at the right time. I played in every Masters from 1964 through 1977. The top-twenty-four rule was a field filler, but I certainly enjoyed it—it worked to my benefit.

---

*One of the negative consequences of Augusta's lush flora and the time of the year in which the Masters is played is hay fever, i.e., allergies. CBS-TV announcer Jim Nantz one year lost his voice to allergies a couple of days before the tournament and had to get some medical aid to be ready to go on the air for the tournament. Former CBS-TV golf commentator **John Derr** recalls the time that golfer Cary Middlecoff was hit with hay fever in the middle of a round:*

Cary had hay fever and a lot of people didn't realize this. How, you may ask, can a golfer have hay fever? I guess it was in '55 that Cary had a good front nine, and I went down to see him going from the ninth green to the tenth tee. He saw me and said, "See if you can find this person" (and he mentioned their name), and then he said, "My hay fever pills are in my car." I said I would go hunt for them, and he said, "Well, get the pills and then come out here and watch because I think you're going to see something." I think he shot the back nine in something like 33 that day.

Now, forgetting to bring hay fever pills is a natural thing for any of us to do while going to play golf. So here's Middlecoff in the third round of the Masters: He's leading it, and he knows if he can get his hay fever pills he can keep it moving. We found the guy who had the keys to his car, got the pills out of his car, got his pills out to him on the thirteenth hole, and he went on to win the tournament. Middlecoff was quite a guy. I did a lot of television with him after that, and we became very good friends.

—◆—

*Masters contestants love the tournament, and they cherish the practice rounds, which can be downright relaxing. It gives contemporary stars a chance to play a round of golf with legends of the game, and the fun sometimes is in seeing who might show up to join you when you least expect it. In his first two years playing the Masters, **Nick Price** got to see the upside of these impromptu practice pairings, as well as the downside:*

In 1985, my second year there, I walked onto the first tee on Monday. I always used to get there on Monday—hit balls around lunchtime, go play nine holes around four o'clock, and then go spend some time on the putting green. It was wonderful because there was no one on the golf course—only about twenty guys. Most of the guys arrive Monday night and then start playing on Tuesday.

I walked onto the first tee with my caddie at around 4:30 to just savor the marvel of Augusta. I was just getting ready to hit when Sam Snead walked onto the tee. He said, "Nick, can I join you?" I was shocked because I didn't know he even knew who I was. I said, "It would be my absolute pleasure, Mr. Snead." We played nine holes. I probably had one of the best nine holes of my life because he's a real character. He told me some stories about Bobby Locke when he went to play Locke in South Africa back in the early 1950s, I think it was. He was seventy-three years old when I played with him that day, but he had a phenomenal memory because he could remember three or four of the golf courses that he had played. Also a great joke teller. More than anything else, I remember on the ninth hole his outdriving me by about fifteen yards. He got one running down the slope, and I hit mine a little high into the wind. I thought this guy must have been something else in his day.

The first Augusta I played in was in 1984 after I had qualified by winning the World Series of Golf. For the first round, I was paired with (1957 Masters winner) Doug Ford, and he is totally the most miserable human being I've ever met in my life. There I was, twenty-six years old or whatever, going to play Augusta for my first time, and I get paired with him. I wouldn't wish that on anyone. He was the most selfish person I've ever played with in my life, and I don't ever say too many bad things about people. He didn't say one word to me and he was walking ahead of me before I hit my second shot, as if I wasn't even on the golf course. But then all of a sudden to go play a practice round a year later with Sam Snead—it was such the opposite. I've played in fifteen or sixteen Masters now, and I have so many memories of Augusta, good and bad, and there's experiences with me and two older guys that were totally opposite.

——⊶⊷——

The week of the Masters Tournament is also a time for family and friends to meet for a festive week in Augusta, usually at the house rented by the golfer whose entry into the Masters is what draws everyone there. In some houses, a family reunion takes place; in others, life becomes a frat party. When golfer **Ken Green** *has played in the Masters, life at the Green house has more resembled the latter:*

The thing I have always appreciated about the Masters is that it was the perfect week for my friends to come, stay, and have a great time. We have so much fun. It's a great week for that: great for them and great for me because I have to cut off the real fun after (Wednesday) to play in the tournament. It's kind of a special wild time because we rent a house or two and just enjoy. The thing my friends appreciate the most is getting them out to Augusta's par-three course and letting them hit some shots. Up until now, we haven't gotten caught. When I go play there, they're allowed to walk around just like the other spectators. When we're pretty sure no one is looking, they'll grab a club and quickly hit a tee shot or a putt. The par-three course is where I really like practicing my putting at Augusta. The greens are perfect, and it's really peaceful out there. That's one of the joys of Augusta.

Another thing we did there during the week was grab a sand wedge and play alternate shots outside around the house, picking out holes all over the yard. It could be a mailbox, a car tire, or even the trunk of the car. We would open it and you had to land a chip in it. We would have a blast. The year we had two houses rented, we were able to play back and forth between them, even using the Jacuzzi or the pool as a hole. At the 1990 Masters, we would sneak into the neighbors' yards for some holes. One day we were getting ready to play, when we looked next door and saw that the people there had posted a cardboard sign that said "O.B." That was a nice way of telling us to leave them alone, which we did. We would also play some hoops. One time we played until about 3:00 A.M. and stopped only when the neighbors called the cops. It's one of those things where you're having so much fun that you don't realize how much noise you're making.

Ron Coffman, *former managing editor at* Golf World, *remembers the days when the magazine would rent an Augusta house for its contingent of writers and editors covering the Masters. One prerequisite: The house had to have an outdoor basketball court:*

It became a tradition of ours that we would invite all the amateurs playing in the Masters that year to come over for dinner one night before the tournament started, usually a Tuesday or Wednesday night. As part of the deal, we would play a basketball game against the amateur golfers, and I remember one year when the amateurs included Curtis Strange, Jay Haas, Craig Stadler, and I think Gary Koch might have been involved, too. It was really an unusual group and we'd be out there trying to kill each other, even before the golf tournament had started. It was pretty good stuff. Some of those guys were pretty good, but of course they were younger than we were, too. The games got very competitive and there was a lot of bumping going on, even though no one really lost their temper or anything like that. Those were fun days.

Over the years, as the technology of the game and the names of the players have evolved, so have the features of Augusta's holes. Every year or so, Augusta officials will alter a bunker, put in a new clump of trees, or some such to subtly change the course. In more than sixty years of visiting Augusta, **Sam Snead** *can see the net result of the slow changes:*

They've been doing something to the course every year. They've made it longer for one thing. Every year at the (Champions') Dinner, we would discuss different things about the course. They've never been satisfied with leaving things alone. For one thing, they built bleachers to enhance the spectators' view at two or three holes. I can remember when they put that trap to the right side of the green at number two. Hogan said, "That damn thing should have been put on the left side." Hogan also once suggested to (Clifford) Roberts something about taking those big fairways and modifying them to make them like U.S. Open fairways. I then asked what they wanted us to shoot, 300? That's why this country is so great—it's always striving to be better. I'm for everything they've ever done.

Golfer **Tommy Jacobs** *was seventeen years old in 1952 when he played in the Masters for the first time:*

I'm still the youngest golfer ever to have played in the Masters. I had gone to the semifinals of the national amateur in 1951 and that's what got me in at Augusta. I stayed in a little trailer near the practice tee, and shared it with Johnny Dawson, another amateur. I was kind of awestruck by the whole experience, but I was fortunate in that I already knew Johnny and that helped make me feel a bit more comfortable. He was an unbelievably nice fellow.

I got to meet Bobby Jones, but I spent more time that week around Clifford Roberts. I got along fine with Cliff. They didn't have a tournament cut in those days. When the tournament was over, they had you go into the club office to tell them what you had spent in expenses that week so that you could get reimbursed. That first year I went in right behind Frank Stranahan. When they asked him how much he had spent, Frank gave them some astronomical figure and they just paid him. No questions asked. So then I went up there and just doubled all of my expenditures, so that I actually made a little money that week. But it was nothing compared to Frank.

—⸺⸺—

*Veteran golf journalist **Al Barkow**'s fonder memories of Augusta and the Masters begin with Gene Sarazen, the 1935 Masters winner:*

Sarazen was always great, even his last year there. He didn't play in the first one because he didn't think it was very important. "I'm not going to go to that little town. And who's Cliff Roberts?" That was classic Gene. I spent five years traveling around the world with him. He was very straightforward. He said that when that course first opened up, it was kind of ratty, in very bad shape with a lot of awful holes. I remember once I went to see (golf-course architect) Robert Trent Jones in his offices and I saw the original sixteenth hole in a photograph—just a little 145-yard hole with a dinky little green with a little ditch across there—a goofy little hole. Then in the forties they redid the whole thing, making it a very attractive hole. Over the years, they've done a lot to that course. It's a beautiful piece of ground, for a golf course.

THE MAGIC

First impressions? It looked different to me than I had expected. The terrain was so much more severe than I had thought it would be. . . .

—D. A. WEIBRING

—◁▥◦▥▷—

Augusta National has been the site and the Masters Tournament the setting for some of the most extraordinary golf shots in history. In only the second year of the tournament, Gene Sarazen struck a shot that was to be heard around the world when he holed out a 220-yard four-wood for a double-eagle two at the fifteenth. That sent him on his way to winning the tournament. The almost-forgotten aspect of that story is that the tournament didn't end when Sarazen's double-eagle shot dropped into the cup. Sarazen still had to come out the next day and beat Craig Wood in a thirty-six-hole playoff.

Magic wands have also been wielded at Augusta by, among others, Doug Ford, who holed out a bunker shot at eighteen en route to winning the 1957 Masters; Jack Nicklaus, who sank a fifty-footer at sixteen on Sunday on his way to holding off Tom Weiskopf and Johnny Miller to win the 1975 Masters; Larry Mize, whose bump-and-run, 140-foot chip shot on the second hole of a 1987 playoff again sealed heartbreak doom for Greg Norman; and Sandy Lyle, whose breathtaking fairway-bunker shot at eighteen in 1988 ended up about ten feet from the hole, from where he made the birdie putt that allowed him to win by one shot.

Augusta magic, however, is much more than just great golf shots and stirring final-hole victories. It is also getting to play the wonderfully challenging yet manageable course when the crowds aren't around and Amen Corner still beckons. It is going inside the clubhouse and having a sandwich in the men's grill or getting access to the Crow's Nest perched atop the clubhouse, which serves as an on-site dormitory room for amateurs who get to play in the Masters. It is driving down Magnolia Lane for the first time and marveling at the beauty and implied opulence, which offers such a sharp contrast to much of the rest of the city of Augusta, where poverty is evident just minutes away. Augusta magic is even pulling a rabbit out of a golf bag, only because a hat wasn't available.

Augusta is not a Disney creation, thank goodness, but it is a special place where people can go to bask in multitudes of great golf moments—moments that can't be generated at will by men, only by men with the willingness amid the right circumstances to make extraordinary things happen.

—◈—

Larry Mize was the proverbial underdog, the third man in a three-way playoff at the 1987 Masters that also included Greg Norman and Seve Ballesteros. Mize was Augusta's Cinderella story, a young man out of nowhere, about to win the Masters, except that Mize's "nowhere" happened to be the city of Augusta. Norman, Ballesteros, and Mize were tied after seventy-two holes of regulation and a sudden-death playoff ensued, in which Mize struck one of the most incredible shots in golf history, knocking in a 140-foot chip shot at number eleven, the second playoff hole, to beat Norman after Ballesteros had been eliminated on the previous hole. For Norman, it was yet another heartbreaking loss under the most unlikely of circumstances; for Mize, it was the achievement of a lifelong dream and an instant boost into the ranks of golf celebrityhood. Mize remembers:

The turning point came on Saturday. I didn't get off to a good start and was two over through eleven holes, going to the twelfth tee. Then I hit my tee shot into the water in front of the green. I dropped about ninety yards back and hit my sand wedge to about ten feet to the right of the hole, and then made the putt for a bogey. It was a huge save for me, and it felt so much better than a double bogey would have. I proceeded to play the last six holes in three under par, including a birdie at eighteen. So instead of shooting something like a 75, I finished with a 72, which got me right back into the thick of things. I remember lying in bed that Saturday night and before going to sleep thinking, *I don't know what's going to happen tomorrow, but I feel really good about where I stand right now. There are some big names in there with me, but maybe I can somehow slip in there.*

I came out Sunday feeling nervous, but nervous is good when you have a chance to win at Augusta. I was

Larry Mize erupts in exultation at the 1987 Masters. (AP/Wide World Photos)

playing with Curtis Strange that day. I think I was one under on the front nine, and when I walked off the tenth tee after hitting my drive there I couldn't help but notice the big scoreboard. I looked up and saw my name up there and kept telling myself, *Quit looking at the scoreboard. You know how you stand; just deal with the scoreboard later on.* I think I then bogeyed number ten. Eleven was key for me on Sunday because I had about a fifteen-footer for par, with the putt on what turned out to be the same line that I would later have for my chip in the playoff. I ended up making the putt there and that reinforced what I would do later with the chip. At twelve, I hit a nice six-iron to twelve feet and made that for birdie. I made another birdie at thirteen, and now I had the lead.

Then came the fourteenth, which has always been a tough hole. I hit my approach a little long, chipped six feet past the hole, and just barely missed the comeback par putt. Standing on the fifteenth tee, I could feel a little breeze in my face, but decided to go for it in two and really ripped my drive. It left me a four-iron into the green, which at the time was the least club I had needed to go for the green in two. I went for the pin and my shot flew over the green and went over into the water by the sixteenth hole. After taking my drop, I ended up having to play a little bump and run, but I didn't hit it hard enough and it stayed short. What that did for me was reinforce the idea that you've got to be aggressive with bump-and-run chip shots like that so you can get it through the rye grass and get the ball running to the hole. And that thought would help me later on, again when I got to the eleventh in the playoff. I ended up making about a three-footer for bogey at fifteen, and while that left me a little down at the time, I was still in it and came back to par sixteen and seventeen.

A memorable experience to my play at fifteen that year was the presence there of a friend of mine, J. R. Carpenter, a tournament official. He saw me hit it into the water and helped me take a drop. He was there again the next year, in 1988, when I was playing poorly—although I had made the cut—and again hit it into the water at fifteen, this time with a three-wood. He again helped me with my drop and I said to him, "J. R., we've got to quit meeting like this," and he said, "You're right, Larry."

At eighteen (in 1987), Curtis was teeing off first and using a three-wood. He hit it perfect, just right of the fairway bunker. I had planned to hit my driver there, but seeing Curtis hit his three-wood, I looked at my caddie, Scott Steel, and he and I kind of just gave it that look that said to switch to the three-wood. So we went with the three-wood and I hit it pure, just next to Curtis's ball, leaving me with a nine-iron of about 140 yards to the pin. I hit it to about six feet. My knees were shaking, but I hit the ball into the hole for a birdie, and that gave me a real boost. Of course, it also put me into the playoff, as it turned out, and gave me a tremendous shot of confidence going into a playoff against two of the best players in the world at the time, Greg Norman and Seve Ballesteros.

I was the local boy from Augusta, sure, but Augusta National definitely was not my home track. I had never really gotten to play there until I first played in the Masters in 1984. I had played it once back around 1980, but that was at a time that they were changing all the greens, and I think I played it when every hole had a temporary green. So that's why I say I never really got to play the course before I made it into the tournament. The excitement I felt was from having such a good chance to win, and I do remember the crowd being behind me. There's no doubt as to who got the biggest cheer when the three of us got to the tenth tee to begin the playoff—me. And that was really cool. We all teed off and I hit it really well, down around the turn. The ball caught a downslope and ended up about twenty to thirty yards past Greg's and Seve's drives. That left me a perfect seven-iron into the green, and I knocked it in about twelve feet underneath and to the left of the hole. Neither Seve nor Greg ended up in a position to birdie the hole and after each had hit his third shot, I had a chance to win with a birdie. I thought it was a right-edge putt, but I didn't give it enough speed and it barely got there. The thing was, though, I didn't want to run it by. I was disappointed, but I didn't want to beat myself up. I still had eleven coming up and Seve had bogeyed ten, so now it was down to just me and Greg.

Greg hit his drive about twenty to thirty yards past me at number eleven, and I was left with a five-iron of about 190 yards. My plan was to start it out right of the pin and draw it in a little bit, but in the middle of my swing I said to myself to keep it away from the water on the left of the green, and I ended up blocking it out to the right a little bit. Greg then hit his second shot onto the green, but it went about fifty feet to the right of the hole, and, at Augusta, it's never an easy two-putt from fifty feet away. So I knew I still had a little bit of life. All I was thinking was to get my chip shot close and put a little pressure on Greg for his first putt. One nice thing about where I was, was that I had only one shot to play—there were no options to think about—take the sand wedge, play the ball back in my stance, and play a little bump and run. The one thing I had to be careful about was hitting it too far and having it go into the water. On the other hand, I remembered the chip I had left short at the fifteenth and knew I still had to be fairly aggressive because I would be landing it short and bouncing it through the rye grass.

It's funny when I look back at the video and see me chip it and then freeze in my follow-through. I wish I could have a front view so that I could see my eyes getting bigger and bigger the closer the ball got to the hole. I didn't know it was going to go in until the last second. Then I just threw my arms up and started running. The thing was, I had to quickly calm myself down because Greg still had his fifty-footer, and if he made it, we would still be tied. When you get into match-play situations like that, you have to assume that your opponent is going to make his shot. I needed to be ready to play twelve if we had to. But I do confess that a little doubt crept in about his making the putt. He then hit his putt, missed it, came over, and shook my hand. All the time, I was a little stunned.

Winning the Masters definitely changed my life. Of course, it was a good thing for me financially. It also gave me a lifetime exemption into the tournament. I also got a lot more chances to play overseas and in outings. In terms of recognition, all of a sudden people knew who I was and they started pronouncing my name right. Yes, people would mispronounce Mize. I would have to tell people it's pronounced the same as size, and just substitute *m* for the *s*. People would pronounce it "Mees" or "Myers." Another thing it did for me was to give me a platform to share my Christian faith, a chance to glorify the Lord.

As I think back, one other thing that helped set me up to win in 1987 was how I had ended up playing in the 1986 Masters. I shot a 65 in the final round to finish in the top twenty-four, which was always a good goal to have if you can't win the tournament because in those days a spot in the top twenty-four earned a player an exemption into the following year's tournament. That 65 is the best round I have ever had at Augusta and it gave me a nice carryover going into 1987.

The three-hole shrine within Augusta National is Amen Corner, consisting of holes eleven, twelve, and thirteen. They are positioned such that a spectator, or patron, can see key shots at each of the three holes with minimal movement required. Golf writer **Herbert Warren Wind** *captured the essence of Amen Corner about as well as any mortal could:*

On the afternoon before the start of the recent (1958) Masters golf tournament, a wonderfully evocative ceremony took place at the farthest reach of the Augusta National course—down in the Amen Corner where Rae's Creek intersects the thirteenth fairway near the tee, then parallels the front edge of the green on the short twelfth, and finally swirls alongside the eleventh green. On that afternoon, with Bob Jones investing the occasion with his invariable flavor, two new bridges across the creek were officially dedicated: one (leading to the twelfth green) to Ben Hogan, commemorating his record score of 274 in the 1953 tournament; the other (leading back to the fairway from the thirteenth tee) to Byron Nelson, commemorating his great burst in the 1937 Masters when, trailing Ralph Guldahl by four strokes on the last round, he played a birdie two on the twelfth and an eagle three on the thirteenth, made up six strokes on Guldahl (who had taken a five and a six on these holes), and rolled to victory.[15]

Melanie Hauser has covered golf and other sports for various publications for more than twenty years, and her first visit to cover the Masters in 1984 couldn't have worked out better in terms of having something nice to write about. That's the year Ben Crenshaw, long a good acquaintance of Hauser's, won the Masters for the first time:

By this time I had gone to work for the *Houston Post* after spending a number of years in Austin, Ben's hometown, writing for the *American-Statesman*. I go to my first Masters and, lo and behold, Crenshaw wins. It was a great experience for me because being at your first Masters is overwhelming in and of itself. But to know the central figure in that year's tournament and to be able to write about the whole week because of that helped ease me in as a writer. It was also a difficult week. Ben's father, Charlie, had told me at the beginning of the week that Ben had made the decision to divorce his first wife, Polly.

But Charlie told me off the record that I couldn't use it until the following week. I knew there had been problems and that there was a difference in Ben's demeanor that week.

During the week I talked one on one with Ben on several occasions. There are times that writers like to talk quietly with golfers that they know well, away from other reporters, and I couldn't do that in a locker-room setting. So one day he and I stood outside the clubhouse in about forty-degree weather and with rain coming down on us. Fans kept coming up to get autographs because I couldn't go into an area where we could get away from it, and that was just part of covering the Masters. I remember walking Saturday and Sunday both with Charlie Crenshaw and how it meant so much to him, not just Ben. The ironic thing about it was that when Ben made the big putt at ten on Sunday, I was going to the bathroom. I ran into a port-a-potty and heard the crowd erupt. When I came out, I asked what had happened and I was told he had made it. I was like, Oh my gosh. I've got to see that one on replay later.

It was great to see Ben win because he had been close to the top at Augusta before. And I knew how much it meant to him to win, especially considering everything that had been going on the week before, with the decision to divorce. I think that kind of lifted him up and enabled him to play a lot better. It's strange—some of his greatest moments have come right after a very emotional time. The second one (when Crenshaw again won the Masters, this time in 1995) was much the same way. He was already at Augusta the night Harvey Penick died. Tom Kite tracked him down. To see him turn that into such a positive thing—it just generated a lot of strength for him. Then you look at the 1999 Ryder Cup also, with Ben as captain of the U.S. team, facing what looked to be a very difficult situation at the PGA Championship, with some players' saying they wanted to be paid for playing in the Ryder Cup. Ben lost his temper, and I've never seen him that mad at anybody in his life. Then he turns around, draws the team together, and wins the Ryder Cup a month later. All those years of knowing him, I knew how much the Masters meant to him, and to see him win it the first time I was there was truly a magical experience for me. I could feel it and it wasn't just somebody I had never really covered winning the greatest tournament ever—it was Ben Crenshaw winning the Masters.

We talked that week about the way he was playing and how he was feeling about his game and his life. I guess about three years before that his swing had been in about a thousand different pieces and he was really distraught—he was in one of those valleys that he goes through. His entire career has been one of peaks and valleys, and he was really down deep in one. I think we just kind of talked about how things were so much better and he was feeling so much better about his game. I didn't broach the subject of Polly with him, despite the fact his dad had told me. I just let it lie. I didn't think it was an appropriate thing to bring up at that time.

Ben Crenshaw's second Masters victory (1995) was even more emotional than his first (1984), coming just days after his mentor Harvey Penick had passed away. (AP/Wide World Photos)

Writer **Dave Kindred** also recalls some of the magic that appeared during the week Crenshaw won the Masters for the first time, as well as some magical moments from other eras:

I can also remember the year Crenshaw won for the first time, in 1984. I can still see him walking from the sixteenth tee to the sixteenth green from my vantage point on the seventeenth-fairway side of the pond. With the sun coming through the pine trees, his hair is alternately gold and dark as the sun hits it. That kind of thing you see all the time there, and it's just kind of a magical place to me. When you used to see Sarazen teeing off first, you'd think, *This is Brigadoon. Time has stopped. This can't be real. Gene Sarazen, 1923, and here it is 1990 or something and he's hitting golf balls. What is happening here?* There's no place like it and I hope it stays this way for another hundred years.

As quick with a quip as any television commentator, CBS-TV broadcaster and Augusta outcast **Gary McCord** *is also an excellent writer with the heart of a poet. Leave it to the subject of Augusta and the Masters to bring out the best in McCord the writer, as evidenced in the following excerpt from an article he wrote for* iGolf:

My next appointment, on my inaugural trip, was with my roommate for the week, Tom Weiskopf. We went over the entire golf course, and he showed me pieces of history as though they were paintings in his foyer. I could see his pride as he told me of past reflections, of his ordeals on this rolling green terrain. Augusta National was awakening his purpose.

My initial response to this rare edition of a golf course was totally sensory. I wallowed in the green of the thing.

The color numbed my soul. There was social order every-where. It was like a giant green operating room. There was no use for disinfectant. The ground and the air were pure in the springtime at Augusta.

The azaleas and the dogwoods were the chrome on an old Buick. They shone as though nature's palate had

A stock photo of Gene Sarazen, "the Squire," shows him lining up to hit a fairway wood, much like he did when he struck his famous double-eagle shot at Augusta in 1935. (Library of Congress)

absorbed a new intensity. The contrast of pine and intense color was mesmerizing. I was on a new level.

—◁▦◁▷▦▷—

While we're on the subject of golf lyricism, perhaps this is as good a time as any to turn things over to Washington Post *columnist* **Thomas Boswell,** *as he waxes poetic about Jack Nicklaus at the 1986 Masters:*

As Jack Nicklaus walked up the eighteenth fairway this evening, the sun was going down on Augusta National Golf Club, just as it is surely going down on Nicklaus's career. The slanting light through the Georgia pine woods lit up his yellow shirt and his receding blond hair. As he and his twenty-four-year-old son Jack Jr., his caddie, approached the green, Nicklaus slowly raised his left hand, then his right, his left and his right again, to acknowledge the waves of joyous ovation rolling from the crowd. In tens of thousands of minds, a camera shutter was clicking. This, among all the photos in the Nicklaus family album of our minds, would be the frontispiece.

First, he was Ohio Fats, then the Golden Bear, and now—finally, most unexpectedly, most sweetly of all—he is the Olden Bear, glorious one last time, walking off the final green into legend with his son's arm around him.

Jack Nicklaus won the Masters today.[16]

—◁▦◁▷▦▷—

Boswell here switches gears from talking about Nicklaus to talking about Augusta itself. Enjoy:

The Masters pleases the eye and flatters the ego of the insider while simultaneously teasing the conscience. Few events in sports offer a richer blend of splendor and pretense. For many, the veranda of the Augusta National represents the end of the social rainbow. There, under a live oak draped with Spanish moss, one can see author Alistair Cooke trying to work up the courage to introduce himself to Arnie. The throngs here, whether they have inherited their tickets or finagled them, bask in the pure self-satisfaction of being at the Masters. Few rewards match a leisurely, rambling week of sniffing the dogwood, ogling the azaleas, lipping juleps, and wandering among the dozen prime vantage points that make this course a unique spectator's heaven.

Nevertheless, always hanging in the background are nagging questions. The shacks along Walton Way near Augusta's downtown, with ragged children and old derelicts in the doorways, are, for many, a condemnation of the pomp along exclusive Magnolia Lane. While silver-haired celebrities sip drinks on the terrace at sundown, an all-black legion stoops to pick up their cigarette butts from the hallowed grass. If Lee Elder needed a crusade to get through the Augusta gates, and if Lee Trevino, the Merry Mex, has felt so uncomfortable here that he has turned down his Masters invitation three times, they are in the minority in more than one sense.[17]

The magic of Augusta and the Masters wouldn't be complete without a story of pulling a rabbit out of a hat, or even a golf bag. Former CBS golf commentator **John Derr** *regales us with this story of the Augusta bunny:*

It rained on Sunday in 1936 and Horton (Smith) won that day. That was the first year they had changed the holes around—they reversed the nines. Horton was coming up the hill to the eighteenth green, and it was looking like he might win the tournament, even though he was locked in a duel with Harry Cooper. Horton had made a sensational chip on the fourteenth hole, so he was in good shape to win it at eighteen. His caddie came over to Horton and he said, "Mr. Horton, we're going to win this thing and we're going to win it right now." Now, this was a rather unusual display of courage and support from a caddie who had been carrying his clubs for seventy-one holes. And Horton said, "What makes you say that, son?" And the caddie says, "Well, if a rabbit's foot is good luck, then we've got good luck and good luck again because we have a rabbit in the bag."

It turns out that when they had been around the fifth hole that day, there were briar patches all around the fifth green. This was a long time back before they really got it looking good around the fifth fairway. This little caddie had caught a baby rabbit and put it in the bag so Horton would have good luck with four rabbit's feet, and he didn't tell Horton about it until they were coming up to the green at the eighteenth hole. Horton was so tickled when he heard this that he nearly blew the tournament there. He had noticed that every time he handed the guy a club to put back in the bag, this caddie would sort of fumble around with it before putting it back down in his bag because he didn't want to poke an eye out of his rabbit. So Horton was the only man who ever won the Masters with a rabbit in his golf bag.

—⟪‹∩›⟫—

Ken Beck has never played in the Masters Tournament and it's likely he never will, although Beck, an author and a reporter for the Tennessean *in Nashville, once accomplished something at Augusta that likely has occurred only a handful of times, if at all. The first time he played Augusta National, Beck birdied all three holes on Amen Corner:*

It was in the spring of 1998. A good friend of mine wanted to know if I could come with him and his father, a member there, to play at Augusta, and of course I jumped at the chance. I have been playing golf since I was ten years old, but I didn't really start playing until I was fourteen or fifteen, which is when I started caddying. I've always enjoyed golf and might be a little better than the average golfer. I've broken 80 a few times, but usually play at around a twelve to sixteen handicap. I'm just a regular weekend public golfer, so this was to be just an incredible opportunity for me to play on such a nice golf course. And when you play on a golf course like that, you've got to have golf shoes, among other things, and have to use a caddie.

Well, this was the first time for me to ever wear golf shoes or to have a caddie. The night before we drove down to Augusta, I went down to Kmart to buy my first pair of golf shoes and spent about thirty-five dollars. It was also a little frustrating because I hadn't played since the previous October. I had been so busy at work that I hadn't even had time to go to a driving range.

We get down there, and I see that it's an unspeakably beautiful place. Green, lush, and sparkling—my idea of golfer's heaven. We played two days even though it was incredible just to play one day. The first day, I was wearing golf shoes and using a caddie for the first time, and that was a different experience. Yet you want to do well when you're playing a golf course like that. I started off playing rather poorly, worse than I normally do. The front nine wasn't a total disaster—I did break 50—but it wasn't very good. I think I shot a 46 or 47. My goal all along was to break 90, which was a pretty big goal.

I've always been a really good putter. I use the same putter I bought in 1967, an Acushnet Bulls'-eye putter I bought for seven dollars, and it's the only putter that I've ever used. If the grass is good around the green, I'll putt from ten to fifteen feet off the green. On the front nine I did putt one in from ten feet off the green and about thirty feet away from the hole.

On the back nine my fortunes totally reversed, which if you play golf a lot you know you can't explain it. Anyway, we turn the back nine, and, again, you use caddies and there's a reason for that. The greens there have such incredible break and speed that you never know what it's going to do without some advice from someone who knows what's going to happen. Number ten is a dog-leg left with a plateau green. I hit a fair drive and it ended up about 190 yards away, from where I hit a five-wood. I hit it just right and onto the green about twenty feet from the hole. The caddie had been telling me all along where to aim it and he had always been just right on. For some reason, the member who invited us gave me a line that was a little bit different, so now it's, Who do I go with for advice on the twenty-foot putt? I went with the caddie's advice on this hole. The caddie told me the same line except for about an inch to the right. I missed the birdie by an inch.

Then we went to number eleven, the par-four. I didn't hit a very good drive and then left my iron shot short of the green and about forty feet from the hole. But my ball was lying on the really nice grass. I wanted to use my putter, so my caddie lined me up and said, "Hit it fourteen feet to the right of the hole," Now you just can't imagine this break. It didn't look like that at all. And then he said, "Hit it about half as hard as you think you need to hit it." So I did exactly what he said, and my ball made a sort of reverse capital C and it just dropped right in the hole for a birdie. Unbelievable.

Then we go to twelve, which is a par-three over Rae's Creek, about 160 yards. The green is cigar-shaped—almost impossible to keep your ball on the green. I think I hit a five-iron just right, cleared the creek with no problem, cleared the bunker in front of the green, and it landed right in the middle of the green. I was left with a sixteen-foot putt, and the caddie said to hit it straight. I did and it went straight in. So now I've got two birdies and I'm thinking, *This is ridiculous*.

Then we go to the third hole of Amen Corner, thirteen, and it's a par-five that doglegs left. I hit a good drive a little over two hundred yards. No way I was going to make it in two, so I hit a three-wood nice and easy, and I end up about a hundred yards short of the green. And this is a really huge green, a long green with many different plateaus on it. The cup had been placed where I believed they have it on the fourth day of the Masters Tournament, where there's just a little plateau. The caddie said, "Now, you really shouldn't go for the pin because it's going to be hard to hold it on the green there," but I said, "Well, hey, I'll try it anyway and go for another birdie." I hit my wedge and hit it just perfectly. It hit on this little table but just kept on rolling right off the back edge, even though I thought it was going to be just perfect. It goes off the back of the green and goes down a small slope into a little swale, about twenty feet from the hole and maybe seven or eight feet from the back of the green.

I told the caddie, "I think I will try to putt this one, too, because the grass is just so nice and closely cropped." He gave me the line on it and told me to aim about three or four feet to the left of the hole. I was probably four feet below the cup. I hit it way too hard, but I hit the line he told me to and it broke just like he said. It slammed into the pin and dropped for my third birdie in a row, all three holes of Amen Corner. If it hadn't hit the pin at thirteen, it would have gone over the green. All of the other caddies just broke out, almost yelling, because they couldn't believe it. They were saying, "How could a sixteen-handicapper come in, playing like a sixteen-handicapper on the front nine, and then birdie all three holes of Amen Corner?" For me, it was just remarkable. In all the years I had played golf I had never had back-to-back birdies, let alone three in a row, and almost a fourth.

I think I ended up with a 38 or 39 on the back nine and I did break 90. We were playing just a fun match with the foursome behind us. So with my sixteen handicap and my par on ten, I was seven under for those four holes. That evening we ate in the clubhouse. We played on a Sunday and Monday, and on that Saturday they had had a members' tournament and most of the members were there. Word got out that a sixteen-handicapper had birdied Amen Corner, so in the clubhouse that night many of the members wanted to come over and shake my hand. I was on cloud nine. I got the member who had invited me to sign my scorecard and had a picture taken with the caddie and all that. I will never top that in my life. That straight putt I had on twelve—I can make that one out of four or five times, but the other two you're just hitting it and hoping it goes in, and you get lucky sometimes. But to do it at this place, this holy ground of golf . . . someone was smiling on me.

I lived an amateur golfer's wildest dream. The members are really proud of this course and they love it when people come in and shoot badly. They take it as an offense when someone comes in and does real well. I think the members were pleased that I did what I did. You know, I could go back right now and tee off a hundred times and never birdie all three. I couldn't do that again if you gave me ten years to do it. That group of caddies said I might have been the first person ever to birdie Amen Corner first time playing it. None of the members knew of anyone else doing it, although there's really no way to know.

Amateurs playing the Masters usually get to spend at least a few days of Masters week up in the Crow's Nest, which is on the top *floor of the clubhouse overlooking the golf course. It's a tad nicer than a dorm room, yet a bit more spartan than a nice hotel room, but no trip to the Masters as an amateur golfer would be complete without at least one night in the Crow's Nest, as **Steve Melnyk** pointed out:*

My first year there (in 1970), I stayed in the Crow's Nest and the next year in a member's room. I ate all my meals there. It would cost a dollar for breakfast, a dollar for lunch, and two dollars for dinner, and it was a dollar a night for the sleeping quarters. That's getting the whole deal for five dollars a day. I remember staying there one year for ten days and getting a total bill for just seventy-three dollars.

To get up into the Crow's Nest, you took a back stairway behind the kitchen. It was like going up into a nice attic, where the sleeping quarters were partitioned off. That was in the days when there was something like ten or twelve amateurs in the field, with the Walker Cup guys there. That's where I got to know guys like Vinny Giles, Lanny Wadkins, Tom Watson, and Tom Kite. We would spend a lot of our time away from the golf course just playing a lot of gin rummy.

---

*Part of Augusta's universal appeal is the familiarity of its eighteen-hole layout, especially the back nine. Television coverage of the Masters has burned Augusta's back nine into the consciousness of hundreds of millions of viewers. Masters participants such as **Sam Snead** can take it one step further, remembering pin placements and putts from across decades of experience:*

Augusta is one of those rare courses where you can remember the holes—after playing it just once or twice, you have no problem with it. To this day, I can remember all the pin placements and how many putts (Ben) Hogan had on each hole when I beat him in the '54 playoff. Oakland Hills is similar in that regard—the holes are distinctive enough for each to have its own memorable identity. I'm proud of the fact that when (Bobby) Jones was asked which was the greatest of all the Masters Tournaments he had seen, he said the Snead-Hogan playoff. I could always raise my game another notch or two for Hogan.

Another dimension of Augusta's magical character are those times when an amateur, a relative unknown, or a PGA Tour journeyman suddenly bursts into the golf headlines at the Masters. Enter **Mike Donald,** *who had won only one PGA Tour event before the 1990 Masters, where he tied a Masters first-round course record with a 64 that gave him the early lead. Donald's quick start at the 1990 Masters is often forgotten because just two months later he made it into a U.S. Open playoff with Hale Irwin, before losing to Irwin while winning the hearts of American golf fans. Donald recalls his opening 64 at the 1990 Masters, at times with a tear in his eye:*

I remember I was playing with Dan Forsman and we had a tee time around 12:30. It wasn't one of the early tee times. My parents were there, my brother was there, and so were some of my friends. I didn't play very well during the practice rounds, and I remember not sleeping well the night before.

I got off to a solid start—I parred the first three holes. And then I birdied four, five, six, eight, nine, ten, and twelve—seven of the next nine. The pin on number twelve was up front, and I had Bill Harmon caddying for me. His father, Claude Harmon, had won at Augusta. Bill is also Butch's brother. He had caddied there a bunch of times with Jay Haas. We got up on the twelfth hole and the wind was blowing a little bit, so I said to Bill, "What do you like?" And he says some kind of a seven-iron. And I said, "A little seven-iron?" And he said, "Well, some kind of seven-iron." He wasn't really sure what to say. I end up hitting it to a foot.

I drove it well on the next hole, thirteen. I was standing out there, waiting on the group in front of us. We had been out there about five minutes, and finally I turned to Bill, and I said, "Billy, you know something? If you had told me this morning that I'd be seven under par after twelve holes, I don't think I would have believed you." And he said, "Well, just don't think about it."

The highlight of the day for me was when I got done and went to the media room, and then after that I went to the range. I was on the far end of the range. I was standing there talking to a few friends of mine and hitting a few balls, and Jack Nicklaus walked onto the range down at the other end. I looked down there and the next thing you know he started walking in my direction. He walked all the way down to the right edge, came over, and shook my hand, and he told me that it was a fabulous round of golf. I thanked him and again he told me how good it was, then he turned around and walked back to the other end of the range to hit balls himself. For me, to have Jack Nicklaus make the effort to walk seventy-five to a hundred yards out of his way to come down there and congratulate me on a fine round of golf was a big thrill and kind of gave me a new respect for him. I mean, when he came down to shake my hand, I was shaking. I had played a good round of golf, but for the greatest golfer of all time to come down there and shake my hand was pretty special.

My final birdie of the day came at fifteen. I drove it okay, but was kind of in between whether or not I could get it there with my second shot, so I laid it up and had about eighty yards. I wedged it to about five feet and I made it. I was now eight under. I can remember at sixteen just trying to hit it to the middle of the green because the pin was in that back-right placement where it's almost impossible to go at it. So I just played for par. On the last hole I hit it into the trees, but hit a hell of a shot just to the left of the green, and then chipped it and rolled it down there right over the lip of the hole, and the ball stopped about six inches away. I then tapped it in.

There were a lot of people out there. It was a bright, sunny day and I was shooting some kind of score. I think I'm always aware of how I'm playing and how I'm shooting relative to the rest of the field. I wasn't really thinking about the course record or anything—I was just trying to get in with a low score. Nine under was the course record, but I was just trying to shoot the lowest score I could. I think I might hold a distinction—I don't know if I can guarantee this—but I might be the only person in the history of golf to lead his first U.S. Open and his first Masters after the first round. My first U.S. Open was in 1984—I shot 68 and was tied for the

For one round in 1990, Mike Donald was the big story at Augusta, as he opened with a 64 to grab the early lead. (AP/Wide World Photos)

lead. But the next day I shot 78, and the next day at Augusta in 1990 I shot 82, so both of them kind of went backward.

I think what happened to me was I came out the next day—another bright, sunny day—about 2:20 in the afternoon, and the greens were really, really fast. They had been fast the first day, but the second day they were extremely quick. I missed a two-footer on the first hole and had it at about five feet above the hole at number two. I remember looking at the grass and it was almost blue. Billy said to me, "Mike, we really need to try to make this, because if you miss it, this could go eighteen feet by." And I remember just tapping it and it went five feet by, and then I missed it coming back. So I had started out bogey-bogey and think I ended up three-putting seven times that day. It was just a deal when I got off to a bad start putting and with the greens really firm and fast, I just got overwhelmed.

Playing in the Masters is something you dream about since you're a kid. I had gone to school in Georgia at Georgia Southern, and we used to go up there and play once a year. For me to have my parents there at the Masters, as well as my brothers, and then to play that kind of a round of golf was pretty emotional for me. It all goes back a long way. My parents were kind of middle-class people, maybe not even middle class. I grew up in a 1,100-square-foot home. My dad was an automobile mechanic and my mom a waitress. They worked their butts off to pay the bills. It was their sacrifices that allowed me to be there. My mother went to my tournaments a lot, maybe eight tournaments a year—the ones in Florida and two or three others, such as Vegas or if I was in a major. She was at my first Open and also at the one when I finished second (in 1990). My dad didn't come very often. As a matter of fact, my dad was a pretty strange guy. I mean he was a great guy, but he didn't like the crowds and he didn't like the fanfare, the attention. He just didn't like it. He said, "It's your stage." When I qualified for the Masters, literally, my dad wasn't going to go, until a week to ten days before the tournament after I had begged him for six months.

Six months after that Masters, my dad and I were just talking when he said, "You know, son, I'm glad I went to that Masters. But I don't think I will ever go again." And the next year when I again played the Masters, he didn't go. Being around all those people and the fanfare made him nervous. To give you some insight into my dad, the next day, after I shot the 82 and I came off the eighteenth green, it was about 7:30 at night and there only were about fifty people left. Everybody was gone and it was misty, and I had shot 82. I came out of that tent and there were about ten to fifteen reporters (including this book's author) standing there by the eighteenth green asking me how I shot my 82—what had happened. I came out of there and answered the questions—and I'm kind of getting emotional now as I remember this, and my parents are now both gone. That night, my dad basically told me that he was more proud of me for stopping and answering the questions like a gentleman after I shot the 82 than he was the day before when I shot the 64. He was more interested in my taking the defeat with some humility than he was when I shot a good score the day before. I did the best I could.

I got maybe one or two letters after all this. Some guy, from Massachusetts I think, wrote me a letter about it, and it was the darndest thing—it was that summer that I opened up with a good first round at the Open. Obviously, round two, I'm apprehensive about shooting a high score again—I had done it before. I go to my locker that Friday morning and see where this guy had left a letter saying, "C'mon, Mike, you can do well, forget about what happened at the Masters and just play well." I got a kick out of it because I'm thinking, *How am I supposed to forget about the Masters when you keep writing me reminding me about it?*

I had only been to Augusta once before while at Georgia Southern, and all I can remember is that I shot a 72 with something like five birdies, and an eagle and seven bogeys. It was a weird round. I did go in and play two practice rounds in March before the 1990 Masters, like a Monday and Tuesday or Tuesday and Wednesday. I have played in two Masters. I missed the cut by a shot the second year. The only thing I remember about that is that I played early on Friday and shot 148, and they had the ten-shot rule. I went back out and was watching Fred Couples, and the leader was six under and I was four over. I was standing there on fifteen and watching Tom Watson hit a three-iron to about ten feet and then make it for eagle to go seven under. I thought, *Well, he could still make another bogey and I'll be in*, but then on the next hole he made about a fifty-footer with ten feet of break for a birdie, and I ended up missing the cut.

These are a few of the moments that mean a lot to me, even if they don't mean much of anything to a lot of other people. The way I look back on my career is, You know what, I wasn't an all-American; I wasn't really a great player in college, and I came from pretty humble beginnings; and I've played the tour almost full-time for about fifteen years and made some nice money with one win and a couple of team championships. When I had started my career, there weren't a hundred people beating down my door wanting to help. I did all right and came out of it okay. I've got some special memories and a few people remember who I am and I made a whole bunch of money. I did okay.

Writer **Herbert Warren Wind** *paints another Augusta master-piece in this excerpt, which originally appeared in the* New Yorker:

It was the prettiest course I had ever seen. In those days, its Bermuda-grass fairways were overseeded with an Italian rye grass that gleamed a lovely shade of green in the sun . . . There couldn't have been more than two thousand people on the course on Thursday and Friday. On Sunday, five thousand at the most were on hand for the final round. It was a treat to be there . . . (T)he players were courteous and approachable. The spectators knew their golf. The pimiento sandwiches at the refreshment stands were fresh and exotic. The clubhouse, an elegant ante-bellum manor house wrapped in wisteria, overlooked the course, and let you know you were in the Deep South as explicitly as did the mockingbirds' song and the abundant flora.[18]

Arnold Palmer *spoke reverently of Augusta National in his 1999 autobiography:*

I remember like it was yesterday, the feeling as I drove up Magnolia Lane into Augusta National Golf Club for the first time. I'd never seen a place that looked so beautiful, so well manicured, and so purely devoted to golf, as beautiful as an antebellum estate, as quiet as a church. I remember turning to Winnie, who was as excited as I was by the sight of the place, and saying quietly, probably as much in awe as I've ever been: "This has got to be it,

Babe . . ." I felt a powerful thrill and unexpected kinship with the place. Perhaps that's partially because Augusta was built by Bob Jones, who was one of my childhood heroes, but also because the Masters, though still a relatively modest event in terms of money, was like a family gathering of the game's greatest players, ruled with a firm, unbending hand by Clifford Roberts. They were all there—Jones, Sarazen, Snead, Nelson, Hogan. Though I'd met them all before, just seeing their names together on pairing sheets or chatting with each other on those perfect putting surfaces was an almost religious experience for me. Privately, I admitted to Winnie that it was like dying and going to heaven.[19]

Part of the charm of Augusta and the Masters is the friendly yet respectful interaction with patrons during the practice rounds. Not all Masters participants take the time to joke with fans, but **D. A. Weibring** *believes it incumbent on him to every now and then give back to Augusta's loyal fans, as he explains here:*

Augusta was one of the first things I thought of the first time I won, which was in 1979 at Quad Cities, to become exempt for the Masters. First impressions? It looked different to me than I had expected. The terrain was so much more severe than I had thought it would be—the contouring, especially of the back nine. How severely uphill eighteen is—I don't think you ever pick that up on television.

As time went on with my playing there a number of times and experiencing that tradition, a couple of things really hit me from the standpoint of the passion and the excitement of the spectators that come each year, especially on Monday, Tuesday, and Wednesday, when you get a really wide variety of first-time attendees. They buy the daily tickets and get out there. You can sense the reverence from the spectators for the golf course and you could really feel that enthusiasm. With it there's a nature of relaxation and fun from the players in the practice round that is enjoyable not only for us, but for everyone. We're not coming in and playing one practice round—we're playing three practice rounds, or maybe just playing a few holes and maybe testing a club or whatever.

Some of the fondest memories I have, and this has happened in a couple of different places, is seeing and talking with fans who always return to their favorite spots on the course to watch. Number-nine green was a place that always intrigued me, especially considering how severe that green is (in sloping from back to front). You get a lot of similar people sitting there year after year back behind that hillside, and they like to watch the players go up and survey the putts. One of the first years I was there, I was up in the back of the green, trying to lag a putt down the hill. I misread it, and it broke the wrong way, ending up five or six feet from the hole. It's a place where you can certainly putt it off the green—a lot of players have in competition.

I turned behind me and saw the spectators kind of bending down, elbowing one another and saying, "I've been watching this putt all day, and it breaks that way and these guys can't figure that out." I looked up and saw this elderly lady, who had probably been coming for years and years. You could tell: She had her pins on and her golf hat, sitting in her chair, pointing. And I said to her, "Are we all making the same mistake?" And she said, "Yeah, they're all breaking that way." So I said, "Well, why don't you come down here and show me how to do it?" So I brought her out of the gallery. At first, she wouldn't move. "I can't do it," she said out of reverence for the place. But I said, "Oh, c'mon," and I kind of got the gallery going, and they all encouraged her, and it was a fun moment where she came down. I gave her my putter, gave her my ball, and said, "There's the pin," and I had my caddie tend it. She putted it right off the green and it went right down into the fairway about thirty or forty yards. And I said, "It's not quite as easy as it looks, is it?" Being a guy who had grown up in a small town, playing public golf most of my life and being fortunate enough to have worked my way to the PGA Tour and to enjoy the fruit of my accomplishment, I knew I was fortunate just to be at the Masters, and I wanted to share something, even in a small way.

Get-togethers at the Augusta houses rented by golfers during Masters Tournament week can be a lot like family reunions or holiday get-togethers. It's one place where PGA Tour golfers such as **D. A. Weibring** *can relax a few days while seeing friends and relatives they don't get to see any other time of the year. Weibring has never won the Masters, although he has been in contention once or twice, but that hasn't taken away from the* *warm fuzzies he has experienced over the years in Augusta away from the course:*

I played well the year Sandy Lyle won (1988). I had a chance. I believe I was two shots back going to the back nine on Sunday. I double-bogeyed ten—missed the green left. But then I came back some and finished seventh, four back of Lyle.

Whenever I went there, we tried to make it that special atmosphere. We'd rent a house and have friends and other people over to visit. And that was special. One time I brought one of my buddies I grew up with in high school in Quincy, Illinois, where I had played golf with him every day. His name is Gary Anders. Gary came down and watched the tournament. Then I would bring other friends, kind of rotate them through. Another year I brought along some college friends, including college teammates of mine from Illinois State.

Remembering all this takes me back to Augusta one year. All golfers who have played in the Masters have their own disaster story from twelve or thirteen. Mine occurred at twelve, where I made an eight one day. And this was after landing my tee shot five or six feet from the hole. The ball skipped into the back bunker and somehow half buried. So I had a little explosion shot there and I hit it a bit too hard. It came out and went down across the green into the water in front. I had the choice of going back and dropping the ball in the bunker, or going across the fairway and taking a drop on that point in line with the tee. I went back across the water in front, dropped, and played the shot. It hit the bank and rolled back down onto the edge of the water. I splashed it back up and eventually made about a six-footer for an eight. I went to the next hole, I'm proud to say, and knocked it on the green in two and made birdie four. But I missed the cut.

That night I'm back at the house with my friends, and one of the guys who was real important to me was a guy named Mike O'Connell, the best player in our area when I was growing up and later the captain of the golf team at Notre Dame. His sons followed him in there and were captain of the team as well. He took me to my first barbecue events, you might call them—little weekend tournaments in the small towns around western Illinois. He was a guy I really looked up to. He won our city championship eight years in a row. That year in which I made the eight, I had invited him to come down along with his two sons, young Mike and Chris. Chris is now caddying for Peter Jacobsen.

Only Mike could get away with this: He was running his video camera, and we had had a few beers at the house, and obviously I was a little disappointed at this point because I hadn't made the cut. Mike turned to me and, with the video camera rolling, said, "Now D. A., which one of those eight shots do you think you hit the best?" He had that laugh and that personality. He tragically passed away a few years later, but I'm thrilled looking back that he got a chance to go to Augusta. He was so kind to me over the years and such a good player, a great influence in my career. Chris still has aspirations of playing the tour.

Renting a house there and having family and friends there really did have the atmosphere of being a holiday season, almost as a little bit of a celebration. I just wanted to share the experience of being at Augusta, which is always so special to anyone who grew up playing golf and loving golf. The first passage of spring, if you grew up in the Midwest, was the Masters and seeing Augusta's beautiful flowers and the golf course and the competition. I've had that. I always tried to prepare the best I could do and compete and do well. Would I have played better if my wife and I had gone there alone and gotten a hotel room and kind of cubbyholed up? I'm not sure. I just enjoyed having people around who were important to me. Later on, with my company Golf Resources, I would bring in some clients and some people I've been working with.

Steve Eubanks, a writer and author of Augusta: Home of the Masters Tournament, *grew up in Georgia and was attending the Masters Tournament long before he ever got his first byline:*

I always remember it as being a much bigger event than anything else going on. Having grown up in Georgia, I always knew that the Masters would be coming around in April and bringing spring with it. As a kid, being able to go to it was one of the biggest thrills you could have, even if you didn't play golf. I didn't play golf seriously until I was fourteen, but every time I went to the Masters I would see these guys and think, *This is what I want to do.* It was one of the most spectacular events you could ever attend. I have since gone to a number of World Series, a couple of Super Bowls, the NBA Championship, and an Olympics, and still nothing can compare to going to that first Masters and sensing the aura of everything going on around you.

The main thing I remember was everything being green. I remember it being so neat that you could go up and buy a Coca-Cola and not get it in a Coca-Cola cup. The complete absence of all other colors really struck me as a child as representative of something special. At most tournaments you look up and see tables, towers, wires and blimps overhead, logos at every corner, and at the Masters you saw none of it. I would go with my father, and it was always a great time. I didn't understand early on the concept of major championships. On our way driving over the first time, I was trying to figure out what the difference was between the Masters and say, the Atlanta Classic or the Southern Open. Dad said, "Think about the U.S. Open." I understood that and said, "Okay, I get it." Then he said, "No, no, this is even bigger." That really made a distinct impression on me and when I showed up I knew what he meant.

———

Augusta officials take great pains to do whatever they can to influence CBS's television announcers to say all the right things about Augusta and the Masters, and to avoid those topics that they would prefer not to be aired, such as mention of money. Television commentator **Steve Melnyk,** *a former member of the CBS team, elaborates:*

When working television at the Masters, there never was a specific requirement to "Do this" or "Don't do that." Working at Augusta National is both the hardest and easiest sporting event to cover. It's the hardest in the sense of being careful to choose just the right words to describe what is going on, yet it's the easiest because the viewer already knows so much about Augusta and the tournament. The trick for an announcer there is to stay out of the way of the telecast. It's one event in particular when silence is especially beneficial: Describe a shot and then keep quiet. A lot of announcers would be better off saying less at the events they are covering. I would say very little, so I had to choose my words carefully.

The things that happened with Jack Whitaker (see chapter 6) didn't scare me when it came to my own announcing, but one thing they made clear was that they didn't want you talking about money. Working the Masters versus another regular event is just different. Like when I go to Kapalua and I'm talking about, say, Tom Purtzer—I will talk about how he won Colonial five years earlier and that's been his last victory, and all that kind of stuff; but if it's Tom Purtzer at Augusta, I'll describe his shot at twelve, then leave it at that.

My best memory of working a Masters telecast was Nicklaus's win in 1986. He orchestrated play on the back nine, shooting a 30 that included a bogey. No one made a move on the telecast without going to Nicklaus first. It was like magic. There was electricity in the air among the spectators. It was the most emotional sporting event I've ever been involved with. It would have been an appropriate time for Jack to retire from golf. He couldn't have ended his career any better than that. We talked about that once, and he said he had thought about it at

the time but decided he loved the game too much to quit
right then.

Golf writer **Melanie Hauser** *recalls Nicklaus's 1986 Masters
victory as an unfolding event of destiny, starting when the
Golden Bear got to number nine. She then segues into her memories of Fred Couples's Masters win in 1992:*

Jack Nicklaus's Masters has to stand out for everybody, I
think. That was probably the most incredible Sunday I
had ever experienced on a golf course, until the Ryder
Cup this year (1999). I was actually out walking with
Tom Kite and Seve Ballesteros, who I think were playing
one group behind Nicklaus.

You kind of get a feeling. Sundays at Augusta, you
tend to walk the front nine with somebody or bounce
around, and then go in and you really have to watch the
back nine unfold on TV because so much is happening
that unless you're out there watching Tiger Woods with
a ten-shot lead, you just can't follow all that is happening. I knew both Tom and Seve well, and besides, I just
loved watching Seve play that golf course. I think he's
magic when it comes to shots around there. I remember
the eighth hole vividly. Kite knocks it up there and gets
an eagle. Seve is off the green, and he goes up and just
kind of stalks the entire green, looking at all the angles
to see where he's going to chip. Damned if he doesn't
come out, hit his shot, and knock it in for eagle. So
there's back-to-back huge roars from eight, and Jack's up
ahead on nine, looking around with a look that says,

"What in the hell is going on?!" And the next thing you know, he makes birdie on nine, and that's what started it for him. At that point, you don't really believe it. He starts to make a move and we're all back in the old press room, a Quonset hut, watching this. We were all gathered around a bunch of TVs, and when he starts making a move it's unbelievable. It's like this guy is ten years old again.

Tom McCollister of the Atlanta paper had written a column prior to the Masters in which he had said to forget about Jack, he's too old to win at Augusta. He may have been one of the guys that called him the Olden Bear, but a lot of us used that term that week. Somebody had given that column to Jack, and he had it taped to the refrigerator in his rented house that week. So we're all kind of laughing in disbelief at what was happening, and with every putt that he made it just kept growing. By the time he made the putt at sixteen, we're all going insane, like "He's going to win this thing!" You hear about the British press going crazy in the press room during the Ryder Cup. Suddenly all these old grizzled writers are whistling "God Bless America" and whooping it up and screaming for Jack. I still get chills just sitting and talking about. It was one of those moments you never expect you'll ever see. We're all stunned and talking about the Olden Bear turning Golden once again. I remember at the end of the night some of the veteran reporters who had covered many more Masters than me were standing up and saying, "This was too big to write," and I'm sitting there thinking that makes me feel pretty good because we're all dumbstruck for words.

When Tiger won, we all knew he was going to win,

and we had time to really think about how to put that into perspective. It was kind of a magic day. You still know when there's a Jack roar out there—I mean you can hear them. You could hear it from within the press room. It all kind of got started with those back-to-back eagles by Kite and Ballesteros at eight—you just knew something great was going to happen. But you didn't know what. It still goes down as the only major I saw Jack win in person. Pretty special to see him come from behind like that, but there are so many other Masters that stick out, too.

Fred Couples's win (in 1992) was amazing. He and I had been on the same plane Monday morning going to Augusta. I get on and I'm back of the bus, and there's not that many people on the plane. And Fred's back there in coach with me. So I go to see him and say, "Hey, how you feeling?" and at that point he's playing better than anybody in the world. He had just taken part of that weekend off to go to the semifinals of the Final Four and hang out with Jim Nantz. And I get around to asking him, "Are you going to play a practice round when you get to Augusta, or what are you going to do?" And he looks at me and says, "I'm going to the grocery store (when I get there) because you've got to have chips and salsa for the Finals tonight." Here's a guy everyone is looking at to win the Masters, and he's worried about getting off the plane and going to the grocery store and getting ready for the game that night. As it turned out, he did come out and play nine holes that day. I saw him and kind of teased him about going to the grocery store and he said, "I'm going after this."

You could see how well Fred was playing, and he was surrounded by a lot of friends of his—an old friend John

Bracken, Paul Marchand—and I walked a lot of holes that week with Paul and John, just talking to them and everything. Paul was talking about how at ease he was. They were watching videos back at home and just having a good time. The boys were just kind of hanging out and Fred was hitting the ball well, and you just knew he was going to put himself into position to win.

I remember walking with Paul the final day and having him say something to the effect that if he's one up or even going into the back nine he's going to win it. At the same time I knew that Fred and Deborah had not been getting along, and that a decision was coming there. I had mentioned something to her about how great it was that all these guys were hanging out, and she was giving me that look and saying "Don't even go there," and I was like, "Okayyyy." He had basically put her out of his mind. I had been at the Players Championship when he won in '84. I remember how relaxed he had been that week, too, with Houston in the Final Four. The first thing he said to me coming off the course that year was, "How're the Cougars doing?" That's a good sign for Fred when he's talking about other things.

In '92 he was on cruise control and so many things were going right for him. To see that shot at twelve that day—to see that shot stay up, it was basically a Velcro shot—one of those shots you've got to have to win a major. I remember talking to Jim Nantz, and he threw his script up when the shot hit, and he didn't even know where it had landed. He was really emotionally involved because he and Fred, along with Paul Marchand, had been suitemates back at Houston. After he had won, I went out to the Butler Cabin and was hanging around talking to a lot of people, and they told me what happened out there after the cameras were turned off. That was when Nantz was sitting in for the presentation at the end of the Masters telecast. Once the telecast went off the air, they just looked at each other, hugged each other, and started crying. It was such a huge moment because it tied everything together. Here were all these people who had sat around in a dorm room at the University of Houston. Nantz would be sitting there and talking about Fred getting the green jacket and it all came together. I remember bringing Paul and John into the press room with me so that they could hear Fred address the media. It was another of those special moments. It was a great thing to see.

—⬤—

THE METHODICAL

As *productive and organized and attentive to detail as they are in the presentation of the tournament and all that, it has put an unrealistic standard on the golfing industry.*

—Tom Weiskopf

Other than the golf itself, there is little about Augusta National that is happenstance. The azaleas around Amen Corner don't just bloom when nature feels like making them bloom, and the water in Ike's Pond isn't a sparkling blue by accident. In the best traditions of club cofounder Clifford Roberts, almost everything at Augusta and during Masters Tournament week is carefully planned and micromanaged. There are no phalanxes of committees that exist for the apparently sole purpose of getting bogged down in petty politics. Autocratic power is the mode of rule around Augusta: That's the way it was when Roberts was alive, and his death in 1978 did nothing to change things. What Roberts said and how he managed things (with an iron fist) still are as much a reality today as they were fifty years ago. Any questions?

Augusta officials' attention to detail is manifested in

what many golfers agree is the best-organized golf tournament in the world, even if it's not the best in terms of strength of fields. The greens are mowed just so; the fairways are precisely manicured; the rules of spectator decorum are clearly explained on pairings sheets; the food is cooked impeccably and never runs out; no running is allowed on the premises; guests can play golf there only when physically accompanied onto the course by members; green jackets are not to permanently leave the premises (unless your name is Gary Player); and recipients of gift notebook planners have been advised to use only a No. 2 pencil. Any questions?

There is method to Augusta's gladness. They are only too happy to show you the door if you choose not to adhere to club customs (as opposed to club policies) and don't bother to ever show up again if you're a club member whose monthly bill suddenly stops coming. Augusta National and the Masters have for decades been run and conducted with a diamond cutter's precision and an accountant's attention to detail (and, for sure, the bottom line, even if they painstakingly and even awkwardly avoid all mention of money). But this is good. It's good because all of this attention to detail, all of this obsessive-compulsive behavior, all of this our-way-or-the-highway mentality has made Augusta and the Masters the shining epitome of all that is good and grand about golf, even if it's not politically correct.

The men at Augusta have their own way of doing things, and as far as they are concerned, the rest of civilized humanity can take it or leave it.

Any questions?

*At Augusta, everything is done according to standards laid out in meticulous detail, to include how CBS-TV's coverage of the Masters is to be handled. Former CBS executive producer for golf **Frank Chirkinian** sums up Augusta's form of government:*

Working with the Masters people has been awesome. I don't think I've ever run into a display of solidarity like that before. There's a total sense of power that has permeated every move we (CBS-TV) have made. It's something that we've all learned to live with. There's always been the sense that they know exactly what they want and, by golly, that's the way it's going to be. And that's good—it eliminates confusion. I learned a lesson in all this: Democratic rule is not an effectual form of government. With autocratic rule, there is no confusion. I became autocratic running the golf coverage. I had to be, because that's really the only sensible way to do things. Pat Summerall even gave me the nickname "the Ayatollah."

---

*Visitors to Augusta during Masters week can't help but be awestruck by what they see—an artist's rendering of greens, blues, reds, yellows, and pinks that make Technicolor pale in comparison. But the aesthetic beauty is only part of the show carefully produced by the green jackets, who also pull out all the stops in presenting one of the most tightly monitored and yet innovative golf tournaments in the world. **Tom Weiskopf** played in many Masters Tournaments and later offered television commentary on the annual golf rite of spring, giving him a discerning eye when it came to seeing how Augusta pulled off this Greatest Golf Show on Earth:*

I enjoyed playing the golf course—it was one of the most interesting golf courses I've ever seen. It's the best risk-reward tournament golf course I've ever played. It was great fun. One thing that struck me was the thoroughness of the attention to detail. What it really did was put golf where it is today. It set a standard. They have worked hard to produce an exciting presentation for the spectator. Consequently, over the years, it has had the greatest impact on what we know as tournament golf today—that and the British Open. Actually, they got their scoring system from the British Open. They just embellished it with things like a lot more scoreboards, bigger scoreboards, and their quickness in putting up scores.

I had a wonderful experience there as a player and as a commentator. The Masters marks the start of the golfing season for most of the world, and the beauty of it makes it all the more spectacular. But there is a negative that has come out of all this, and it's what I call the Augusta Syndrome. As productive and organized and attentive to detail as they are in the presentation of the tournament and all that, it has put an unrealistic standard on the golfing industry. I've seen guys walk in there from Bangor, Maine, or wherever with their chairman of the greens committee or superintendent and say, "This is what I'm talking about. This is what we need at our facility, all these beautiful flowers and everything."

Everybody forgets that Augusta has the luxury of conducting a golf tournament for which it is able to spend whatever is necessary to produce whatever they want to produce. They make changes all the time. There is a perception, difficult to achieve and difficult to overcome, that it is the finest-conditioned golf course in the world. Well, let me tell you, there are a lot of golf courses, on a daily basis, that are in as good of condition and even more so throughout the year than Augusta National. I have been there well before the tournament and well after the tournament, when the dye isn't in the water and

Tom Weiskopf came close a number of times to winning at Augusta, but he could never quite pull it off. (AP/Wide World Photos)

167

that red Georgia clay turns the water to off color—when the azaleas aren't in bloom, when the spectators aren't there, and when the excitement of the tournament isn't there, and it just isn't the same Augusta National people are accustomed to seeing on television. Anyone who uses that Augusta they see for one week out of the year as a model for what they want to do with their own club is setting unrealistic standards for how their own course should look. I say forget all that aesthetic stuff and put your time and money into your golf course itself, and make it the best it can be.

Jack Nicklaus has won six green jackets, more than any other golfer in history, and he sees Augusta and the Masters as much more than just another major-tournament conquest for him:

It is hard to imagine that there has been a good golfer since the Masters Tournament began in 1934 who hasn't dreamed of winning it . . . Young as the Augusta National is relative to how long the game of golf has existed, it exudes more history and is home to more ghosts than any other American golfing mecca, to a degree that still pumps me up just driving down Magnolia Lane each April. Part of the appeal is the way the Masters has set the pace in providing the finest quality and condition of golf course and the highest standards of tournament organization and presentation. Many of the refinements and special touches we enjoy today all over the world as players or watchers of top tournament golf derive from the Augusta National and the Masters. It would, for instance, be foolish of me to deny that they were and remain the inspiration and model for the golf club and the competition I started in the mid-1970s, Muirfield Village and the Memorial Tournament.[20]

―――――

One of the best-kept secrets in America is the membership list at Augusta National. What is known is that the club's membership numbers around three hundred and includes some of the most powerful CEOs in America, but they comprise a list that isn't for sale to telemarketers, for sure. Even **Sam Snead,** *who's as closely associated with Augusta and the Masters as any living golfer, doesn't know who belongs, and he doesn't ask:*

I couldn't name you five members at Augusta. They aren't at the (Champions') Dinner, and they don't come to the clubhouse while the tournament is going on. And I've never been curious to know who they are. But I gave the club my one-iron one time and it has been displayed, so I know they appreciate me.

―――――

Ken Green, *a PGA Tour veteran known as an antiestablishment guy, has never been a particularly good fit at Augusta:*

The only problem I've ever had with the employees at the club is that they kept calling me sir. As for the green jackets, they're pretty stuffy. They won't say hello to you unless you say it to them first. But I was ready for that because people had told me to expect it. The only other club I've been to that is at all similar is Westchester (near New York City). It makes no sense to me to treat people that way. It's not like the Masters Tournament is being forced on the people at Augusta—it's their choice to have it. I mean, it's not like the U.S. president came in and insisted that Augusta be used as the venue for the Ryder Cup. Why pretend that you're better than anyone else? A lot of their members are CEOs who run corporations that are involved in charity work and public image. Then again, maybe Augusta is their way of getting relief from the baloney they go through at work.

The rise of televised golf and the Masters Tournament have run concurrent to each other for more than forty years, and it's conceivable to think this has all been manufactured by the green-jacket likes of Bobby Jones and Clifford Roberts, sometimes in subtle ways, sometimes not. Former CBS-TV commentator **John Derr** *says there were two other men who played a big part in bringing Augusta and the Masters to the forefront of the American consciousness:*

Television changed a lot of things for a lot of people. TV was a great impetus for getting the Masters into the forefront of the American public. But you had some personalities that did that, too. You had a man named General Eisenhower and a man named General Palmer, and with that many generals around, there were a lot of us privates who thought golf was a great thing.

Arnold Palmer's streak of winning the Masters in even-numbered years was stopped at four in 1966. (Library of Congress)

In the early days of covering the Masters for television, **John Derr** *and his cohorts had to rely on some good old-fashioned American ingenuity for making things happen, like getting scoring updates on golfers about to enter the coverage area at the fifteenth green:*

You know what our communication system was at that time? I was at fifteen, doing the fifteenth and sixteenth holes. We had no radio communications, no telephones, no shortwave, no Internet or what have you. What we did was make up little sheets of paper that had the names of each two-player pairing that day and had one of the members of Augusta National—wearing his green jacket—who would volunteer to stand by the green at the fourteenth hole. When the players had finished fourteen, he would write down Snead minus-2 and Hogan minus-3 or whatever their score was through fourteen holes for that particular round. The man in the green jacket would then give the piece of paper with the scores to the son of one of the caddies we had hired to run the scores. The caddie's son would be standing by, and he would be given this piece of paper and told to "Beat your tracks down the rough, go around the pond, and get over to the fifteenth tower!" At the fifteenth tower I would lower a clothesline down with a snapping hook on the end of it. And this kid was to put the piece of paper in the clothespin, and I would pull it back up.

By this time the players who had left the fourteenth green and for whom we had the scores, would be coming down the fifteenth fairway, and I would be able to say with a great deal of assurance, "Here comes Snead and Hogan, and Snead is two under for the day and Hogan is three under," and people would wonder, *How in the world does he know that?* This worked fine one time in rehearsal before we went on the air. Then the second group came down and there was no caddie's son and there was no paper. So I had to ad-lib what these people had done. It wasn't going out, only to the control room, so it really didn't make any difference what I said, so I gave them some mock scores and talked about them a little bit. As soon as rehearsal broke, I looked around to see where my caddie's son had gone. I finally looked over at the pond behind the fifteenth hole, and here's this little boy sitting on the side of the pond, simulating that he has a fishing pole in his hands and every few minutes he jumps up like he's just had a bite on the fishing pole. So I shimmy down the pole, go over to him and say, "Son, where are the other sheets? You didn't bring me but one."

"Well," he said, "my daddy only caddies for one group at a time." He thought that that was his day's work, that we were going to give him fifty cents for bringing that one piece of paper down. Anyway, I got him straightened out, and we were able to get the scores. As far as I know we had them fairly accurate.

As an amateur playing in his first Masters, **Jack Nicklaus** *had a particular method for getting the most out of his week at the Masters—eat now and pay later:*

To shake off the cobwebs of the long Ohio winter, I had obtained permission to spend time well ahead of the (1959) Masters practicing at the Augusta National. In those days amateur contestants were accommodated for free in the Crow's Nest, a sort of dormitory at the top of the clubhouse. Also, chiefly to protect their amateur status, I suppose, they were charged only a nominal rate for meals—as I recall a dollar for breakfast, a dollar for lunch, and two dollars for dinner. The only person I know who enjoys eating more than I do is Phil Rodgers, and he also had decided to get in some early work on site that year as an amateur Masters invitee. Immediately after golf (each day), Phil and I would hasten to the dining room, where we would begin with a double shrimp cocktail, then each polish off a couple of sirloin steaks with all the trimmings, then if we felt like it, go on to a third steak. This lasted for a couple of days, whereupon someone decided to change the rules. "Fellas," Phil and I were told, "if you're going to eat more than one steak every night, we're going to have to charge you another two dollars apiece for the extra ones." That slowed us down a little bit, but not much. Like everything else about the Augusta National, they were great steaks.[21]

—————

Over the years, Augusta officials have occasionally solicited opinions from Masters contestants about how they can tweak their course into making it better. On the other hand, some suggestions have come unsolicited, although it depends on the source as to whether or not his suggestions will be listened to. **Arnold Palmer** *was one of those so favored at Augusta, as he explains:*

I was pleased when around 1965, Cliff invited me to make suggestions about how the golf course could be improved. My actual belief was that there wasn't a whole lot to do—that Alister Mackenzie's wonderful design ought not to be tampered with very much. For such a sturdy guardian of tradition, some of the changes Mr. Roberts said he wanted to make surprised me. For example, he wanted to create a new lake that would stretch almost the entire length between tee and green of the par-three fourth. But I argued that such a lake in that spot simply wouldn't fit the tradition of the course. He accepted that argument and the lake was never built (and I hope it never is). He also wanted to switch the greens from Bermuda to bent-grass surfaces, and I wasn't a bit keen about that idea, either, because it would drastically alter their character, in my view. Bermuda is a tougher, coarser grass that causes a ball to bounce slightly when it lands. Part of the challenge of hitting a ball onto a green at Augusta National was allowing for the tricky undulations of the putting surface.[22]

---

*When Bobby Jones and Alister Mackenzie designed the Augusta National golf course, they wanted a course that would test a pro golfer's shotmaking and course-management abilities while yet being a course that could be easily enjoyed by amateur golfers of higher handicaps. One of Mackenzie's guiding principles was designing a course where four would be "par" for each of the eighteen holes, although, officially for purposes of the scorecard, there still would be a mix of par-threes, par-fours, and par-fives. So what does it take for a Masters contestant to manage the Jones-Mackenzie creation? For the answer to that, writer Thomas Boswell once called on **David Graham,** among others, to discuss shot strategy at Augusta:*

Of all the courses in the world, Augusta National places the most emphasis on strategy and is the best example of what a major is all about. Every shot here offers an option. That's the key. You've always got a safe side of the fairway or the green to aim at, where you know you can find your ball sitting on short grass. But from those safe spots, you are not, by any means, guaranteed par. From the wrong sides of the fairways, you have much tougher approaches and then from the safe sides of the greens, you put enormous pressure on your putter. Caution here is an invitation to make bogeys.

On almost every shot, there is also a more dangerous shot available that promises greater rewards. But those shots also invite double bogeys. So every hole can be played cautiously with the probability of making par but the danger of getting jittery and making bogey. Or you can risk real trouble but have a good chance for birdie.[23]

As far as course design at Augusta goes, sixty years of a change here and a change there have, in total, evolved a golf course that prompts **Tom Weiskopf,** *also a veteran course designer, to wonder if it is remaining true to the vision Mackenzie and Jones brought to it:*

I liken Augusta, the golf course, to a cadaver that's being used in a medical class. And the disappointing thing to me is the fact that it has been changed so much since I first played there (1968) that, like the cadaver that's getting worked on constantly by future surgeons, there's a chance that some of the golf holes at Augusta will become almost unrecognizable in the future. It's just gone through years of change. What's been done for the most part, I just don't agree with—architecturally, strategically, and conceptually. If they had just left it alone and just added length, they could have accomplished a more palatable presentation.

Any golf course, as it matures, either through vegetation, tree growth, or improved turf conditions and grass that gets better over time, becomes prettier. If, indeed, Alister Mackenzie was as respected as an architect as I think he should be, then why do they do things that are so contrary to Mackenzie's designs? Start with the first hole. When I used to play there, there used to be a little bunker on the right side of the fairway and set into the face of the hill. Its purpose for being there was directional. It was not a penal, strategic bunker; it was a directional bunker easily carried from the tee, giving players the proper line from the tee to play at the right-hand side of the hole, thus affording the opportunity to play to any of the four championship pin placements. But then they came in there and lengthened and enlarged the bunker, making it almost impossible—unless you were the longest of hitters—to drive up the right-hand side on the preferred line to play into the green. That changed the character of the hole. I totally agree, however, with the planting of the ten to twenty trees on the left-hand side. Those new trees offer a beautiful change that looks natural. But they went against Mackenzie's philosophy by changing the bunker, in the process making number one the most difficult driving hole on the golf course.

I could go on for every hole. Let's talk about the third hole. The original philosophy of how to play the hole was eliminated with a series of chop-and-drop bunkers and mounds. The original concept was that if the pin was on the right half of the green, you drove to the left half of the fairway. And if the pin was on the left half of the green, you drove to the extreme right side of the fairway. What Mackenzie was doing there was giving you a false sense of security off the tee—the fairway was so wide that you couldn't miss it. In its original form, the third hole offered much more of a challenge to the golfer trying to get the left half or the right half of the fairway because of the enormous width that he presented. What was done to change it doesn't even look like what Mackenzie would come close to doing.

To simplify it, what has been done is so contrary to the original Mackenzie layout that it has really ceased to be an Alister Mackenzie golf course. My cadaver analogy is a good one. Maybe ten or twenty years from now, if I'm still around watching the tournament, these holes will become unrecognizable compared to what I remember them to be. It's pretty simple—they're worried about score.

My first time there was in 1968, when they had Bermuda greens overseeded with rye grass. Those were very firm greens. The contours for the most part were more severe than they are now, but the putting surfaces weren't as fast. But I thought they were better surfaces back then. Since they changed to bent, whenever that was, I've seen players hit their ball at the eighteenth hole to the pin in back of the green on the top and have the ball spin back all the way down to the front of the green, eighty or ninety feet. That never happened with the

Bermuda-based greens. The ball didn't spin back like that; it usually went forward.

—◆—

*According to **Weiskopf**, there has been at least one time when a great player-designer was consulted about a design change at Augusta, only for the design to not come off as designed. That player-designer was Jack Nicklaus:*

Without a doubt the greatest player I've ever seen compete in the game is Jack Nicklaus. One time we were doing a Masters preview show a couple of weeks before the tournament, and (Frank) Chirkinian had Jack come in there and he's going to do some segment at the sixteenth hole, trying to make the same putt he made in '75 to beat Johnny Miller and me. Jack stood out there for a long, long period of time and never made the putt. And he's getting a little frustrated, understandably. So Frank says, "Why don't we take a break here," and Frank came down to me and said, "Tom, have you seen the new change at the thirteenth hole?" And I said, "What?! They changed the thirteenth hole?!" And he said yeah, and I said, "No!"

Frank and I get into a golf cart and we drive over there. They had changed the green and had put in this big swale behind the green, and they had redone the bunkering and all this and that. Frank says, "What do you think?" And I said, "I think this is going to be very controversial. The players aren't going to like it."

So we drive back and I'm having lunch, and Jack walks in. We started talking and he said, "Have you seen the change at thirteen?" And I said, "Yeah, I've just been down there."

"What do you think?"

"I totally disagree with it, and I think it's going to be extremely controversial—I don't think the players are going to like it."

"Are you kidding?"

Jack got quite a puzzled look on his face, and then he said, "Take me down there." So we got into a golf cart and drove down there onto the other side of Rae's Creek, the fairway side, just mid-green. He stood up in the cart, threw his arms up, and he had a very, very surprised and kind of dumbfounded look on his face. I said, "What do you think?"

"Well, that isn't what I told them to do."

I said, "You didn't even see the change? Your company did it and you weren't even here?"

"Oh, I drew it out for them and I told them what to do, but this isn't even close to what I told them to do."

"You weren't here?! Jack, you know what, I guess now we ought to change the sixteenth hole at Cypress or the eighteenth at Pebble."

As I predicted, the players played it and they disliked it. And it was changed back somewhat. But why change it (in the first place)? The reason, I was told, was for drainage purposes coming off the hillside down to the creek. Well, I know enough about design to know that you could have cut a swale in behind those azalea bushes to stop most of the drainage problems. But I think they got worried about too many eagles and giving away too much crystal. The green contour didn't even resemble the old Mackenzie green. It was just out of character.

If my company had been asked to make changes at Augusta, I would have declined in changing anything at all concerning the thirteenth hole. Another important thing to me is that I had always looked at the thirteenth hole as a psychological hole in the golf tournament. In other words, if you don't make a four on that hole, you felt like you lost a stroke or more to the field. It used to be you always went for the thirteenth green on your second shot if you had a three-wood or less in your hand. Now, you don't go at it unless you have a two- or three-iron or less in your hand. The risk-reward factor isn't what it used to be, and it's now just another par-five hole instead of being a strategic and psychological hole. To me, Alister Mackenzie had a great golf hole, but what exists today is not in the flavor intended for that hole. Since then, they've taken the depth and severity out of that swale they had put in behind the green, and they softened the green a little bit. By the way, Jack finally did make his putt at sixteen for the Masters preview show, after lunch.

———

Other recent changes at Augusta have gone over like a lead balloon with veteran golfers other than Weiskopf. Three-time Masters champion **Gary Player,** *who won his first green jacket nearly forty years ago, still plays, and occasionally still jumps into the periphery of contention. Player criticizes the change made at seventeen before the 1999 Masters, in which a new tee was inserted to make the hole play significantly longer:*

Augusta is a place of beauty—it captures the joy of spring, and it's wonderful to see how all of those trees have grown through time and to see all the improvements they have made on the golf course over the years. I just hope they don't start getting too carried away. The change they made at seventeen is not something I'm crazy about. I think they've really hurt the golf course with that. They've gone about it the wrong way. The hole was designed for the green to receive no more than a six-iron, and now some days with the wind in your face, golfers are hitting a three- or a four-iron for the second shot. Bobby Jones, Clifford Roberts, and (Alister) Mackenzie did not design the course for that kind of shot. The seventeenth hole has been ruined.

The Masters Tournament by far has the smallest field of any of the four major tournaments. For years it has maintained strict criteria for determining which golfers get an invitation and which don't. The Masters field typically numbers well under a hundred, usually in the eighties, meaning there are always deserving golfers who don't get in. One year it might be a Tom Kite, the next a Greg Norman. But that's just another charm of the Masters, which offers an intimate setting that on a good day could be described as cozy. Depending on which side of the pond (the Atlantic, not Ike's) you reside, the Masters either lets in too many foreign-born players or not enough. Back in the late 1980s, when the Sony World Rankings were starting to lay down roots of credibility, party lines were split between whether the rankings should be used as an invitational criteria or not. Augusta officially added the World Rankings to its criteria in the late 1990s, but back in the late eighties it was a hot topic being addressed by **Hord Hardin,** *then the Masters Tournament chairman, as he points out here in a quote that ran in a 1989 edition of the* Fort Worth Star-Telegram:

Although we don't go by the Sony rankings, I look at them because they tell me a lot. But I'm not going to be bound by the Sony rankings. We've used our good judgment over the years and damn little fault has been found with it. We try our damnedest to keep the field at eighty, and this leaves us with very few invitations to give players who can't otherwise get in.

Even if you disagree with how Augusta and tournament officials run their show, chances are your opinions will never be heard. That goes back to Augusta's autocratic rule, which didn't end with Roberts's suicide in 1978. **Curt Sampson,** *author of* The Masters, *had that point drilled home to him while he was researching his 1998 book:*

What was brought home to me by seeing it and experiencing it, was that it's a privately owned club and a privately owned major golf tournament. I assumed the Heisman Trophy is privately opened. The PGA Championship is something owned by this sporting organization. But the USGA and R&A give you the impression that they are more public, or democratic, institutions. The Masters doesn't even begin to try to give this impression. That's okay. They think of themselves as protectors of the game, one-quarter of golf's majors, and they're golf nuts and I have sympathy for that. What I don't care much for is their attitude. A lot of people in sports bureaucracies are like that. For instance, you call the league office for the NBA and people act like they own basketball, which of course they do not. A few people who rise up in golf bureaucracies, and the Masters isn't alone—I would also include the USGA, the R&A and the PGA of America in this—they start getting this proprietary attitude that it's their sport, their game, and their championship, and people not on the inside are, to them, a bit intrusive. That can be a real pain.

Sportswriter **Dave Kindred** *has covered numerous major sporting events around the world, giving him a broad perspective from which he can evaluate the Masters against the backdrop of other major sporting events of its ilk:*

It's different from any other sports event I've covered. The Masters is closer to maintaining its original identity than any other sports event in the world. That's because they alone, the Masters officials alone, have resisted the impulse to take all of television's money. They take some of television's money in return for control of their event. That's why supposedly only the back nine is shown, although television has found ways to show you much of the front nine. That's why there's no network promos during the telecast and a limited amount of commercial advertising—like half as much as could be expected. That's because Augusta has not extorted every last cent from television. Television, therefore, doesn't have to make as much money. There is no commercial signage on the course, even to the extent that Coca Cola, the sacred elixir of Atlanta, has its signs on the soft drink machines taped over. Even at Wimbledon, you see Rolex at center court, above the match clock. There's no Rolex at Augusta. There's nothing, just a golf tournament.

There's a great dignity and honor to that. At the same time, while I say it's my favorite sports event ever and the one I most look forward to every year, it's kind of a guilty pleasure because there is no doubt that it's a plantation mentality. There's a paternal feel there. Brown vs. the Board of Education hasn't quite taken effect at Augusta National. I once wrote for *Golf Digest* opposing points of view about Augusta, the heaven and hell of it. I argued both sides, but I did say that the person writing the "Augusta National is hell" piece was not Dave Kindred—it was his evil twin. You can make arguments either way and I come down on the positive side. It's a great thing for golf. It's a great thing for sports. It's a great thing just for the integrity of sports.

Augusta alone still stands now for what it stood for in 1935, and that's not easy to do in today's world. Plus it's just a beautiful place. I just love to be there. Mac O'Grady one time made something like an eight or an eleven on a hole there. When he came off the course, his explanation was that he had been "overcome by the biophelia." So I asked, "Mac. *Biophelia?* Define that." And it turned out to be the perfect word. It's the feedback you get from your biological surroundings, and he said that there was just too much of it. And there is. At Augusta, everywhere you look, it's a beautiful landscape. It's a painting everywhere you look.

Another time, I wrote one of those Wednesday-for-Thursday columns, and I didn't know what else to write. So I went out to the third fairway and I ended up writing about a guy riding a tractor, just mowing the fairway. I was so entranced by what he was doing. There was this pattern he was cutting into the grass, and with the sun coming down just right through the pines and with the shadows and that, it was just beautiful. I tried to interview this guy, and he wouldn't talk to me because he couldn't—it was against the rules.

—⟨⟨⟩⟩—

Renting a house during Masters week is an expensive proposition, but it has become practically a necessity for golfers in dire need of a feeling of down-home normalcy during what otherwise is an out-of-body-experience week. **John Feinstein** *explains Augusta housing in his book* The Majors:

Once the Masters is underway most players get into a routine that is almost identical every night. Few of them venture into Augusta's restaurants, in part because the town isn't exactly San Francisco (there is a note on the inside of the menus at the local Red Lobster informing customers that they are dining in the place selected by Augusta magazine as having "the best seafood" in Augusta) and because any player who is the least bit recognizable will have a tough time getting through a meal without getting writer's cramp from signing autographs.

So most stay in. Everyone brings friends and family to Augusta. Since just about every player in the field rents a house (standard price for the week is $5,000 to $8,000 unless you choose to go really upscale) there is usually plenty room for everyone. Some players go so far as to rent two houses, one for those in their entourage who want to stay up late, the other for the golfer, who needs a decent night's sleep. Olin Browne, playing in his first Masters, had done that. "We have the frat house and the house of sanity," he said. "I'd love to hang out in the frat house more, but I can't."[24]

———⸎———

Phil Harison has been Augusta's first-tee starter for the Masters since 1947, and his is a position of responsibility sensitive to golfers' nerves:

My job is to make the players as comfortable as I can. Walking on the first tee here is a very nervous moment for most of them. I talk with them if they want to talk, leave them alone if they want to be left alone. But I try to keep the introductions short and sweet. The people here know who they are and what they've done. They just want to get on the first tee and get the first shot down the fairway. They don't need me holding them up by reciting their life history.[25]

———⸎———

THE MOB

Augusta is somewhere you really want to be because of the little quirks and because of the differences and the peculiar little southern ways which still exist—some of them are good, some of them bad.

—MELANIE HAUSER

This chapter is dedicated to Jack Whitaker. Jack didn't ask for this, and he wasn't nominated by any board or committee. But he earned it, in keeping with the great traditions of Clifford Roberts and Augusta, by author's autocratic decree.

Whitaker, you might remember, is the bellwether of television-sports commentators, a keenly observant essayist, who at one time was one of the biggest names in television sports, even before Howard Cosell crashed the party. At one time Whitaker was CBS-TV's golden boy at the Masters, until one day in the 1960s, when he was unceremoniously canned by the network, allegedly for his use of the term *mob* in describing a crowd of spectators who rushed the eighteenth green near the finale of the tournament. A recent book about Augusta and the Masters, researched with the club's blessings, claims that

Whitaker's removal from the CBS Masters announcing crew had little if anything to do with his verbal gaffe, but Whitaker in his own 1998 book insists that his verbalized "mob" was his quick ticket out of Augusta. Even Frank Chirkinian, CBS-TV's longtime executive producer for golf, echoes Whitaker's account. Feel free to draw your own conclusion.

According to *Merriam-Webster's Collegiate Dictionary, Tenth Edition*, the first two definitions of the noun form of *mob* are (1) "a large or disorderly crowd; esp: one bent on riotous or destructive action"; (2) "the lower classes of a community: masses, rabble." Certainly, that doesn't sound like the Augusta-Masters we all know and love. In another vernacular, *mob* refers to gangs, or more specifically, organized crime, i.e., the Mafia. Keep in mind that official Masters television guidelines even preclude the use of words such as *fans* or *spectators* to describe those ticket-bearing people who watch the Masters. The proper reference for such customers is *patrons*. Patrons can't possibly comprise a mob.

Often by circumstances beyond their control, media members covering the Masters Tournament have occasionally become the news story themselves. The most notable of these unwitting participants in Augusta-Masters lore are Whitaker and Gary McCord, another CBS commentator, who almost thirty years after Whitaker met his Waterloo at Rae's Creek after using references such as *body bags* and *bikini wax* to describe the action on the back nine. Announcers, commentators, writers, and authors—journalists all—have experienced Augusta and the Masters to the hilt, and they offer their own wide range of observations and anecdotes to round things out, with a quick aside from Doug Sanders tossed in to add a little color to the mix.

Notice, too, that the exponential growth of interest in Augusta and the Masters has resulted in an on-site media contingent that is as big as some of the galleries in the early days of the tournament. Everywhere you turn at Augusta during Masters week, there is someone holding a pad and pen or a microphone, and they number in the hundreds, speaking in at least a half-dozen different languages. This is the greatest Augusta irony of them all: The media has become the mob. Somewhere, Jack Whitaker is smiling.

Frank Chirkinian, who ruled CBS-TV's golf coverage for nearly forty years, offered this take on the respective Jack Whitaker and Gary McCord episodes that led to each getting removed from the CBS team for Masters telecasts:

It (the Whitaker incident) occurred on a Monday. There was a good number of spectators out there that day using passes they had gotten from regular ticketholders who had left after the seventy-second hole the previous day to return to work or whatever. It was an unruly scene when they came to eighteen on Monday, with the crowd bursting forward to rush toward the green. Whitaker, who was in the tower at eighteen, at that point said, "Here comes the mob!" We didn't have any immediate reaction to what Jack had said because everyone knows exactly what he was describing. It was quite true, but it was one of those things that all broadcasters need to learn—there's no reason to say anything when the television picture is already telling the whole story. Describing it is only redundant and is better left unsaid. It's like when some members of the print media criticized us in 1996 for not saying on the air that Greg Norman was choking. That really ticked me off. I mean, why say it? The viewers could see for themselves what was happening.

As for Gary (McCord), he said something he shouldn't have said. But that's his way of being different. He was talking about an approach shot that went over the seventeenth green, and instead of saying, "If you go over the green, you're dead," he used the euphemism about body bags. I flinched when I heard that because, yeah, it was kind of an insensitive remark. In retrospect, it was kind of funny, but it wasn't then. The body bag remark was more objectionable than the bikini wax reference he used at another point. I don't even know what bikini wax is. What Gary did ultimately created a hardship for the production of the Masters telecast. That was just one more experienced guy that I couldn't use. Then I lose Ben Wright and Pat Summerall. It was like losing the whole announcing crew. We all hope that Gary can come back to the Masters, but I don't know how long his sentence is for. I'd like for him to have a chance to come back just like I would hope that Ben Wright can come back, period. Gary does have a tendency to rant and rave, but he's a pretty good telecaster who brings something good to the production, and I prefer that to a guy espousing a bunch of vanilla all day long.

McCord wrote his response to the "body bag–bikini wax" debacle in a 1994 Golf World *column titled "I Can't Argue with the Masters." Here's an excerpt:*

In a world hungry for stink, this appears to rival Al Bundy's socks. There are stentorian bellows of foul play and censorship. Censorship is a very gray area when dealing with a democratic society, vague at best. In an autocratic society such as the Masters, there are no censorship laws. These people run the most prestigious tournament in the world, copied by all who view its efficiency and stature. They have got it right, and they control it right down to when the azaleas and dogwoods bloom.

I applaud their decision. In the contract with CBS, they have the right to evaluate the announcers and decide who personifies the muted rituals of restraint. I am a loud wail. They are doing what they think is in the best interest of the Masters, and I can't argue with the decisions they have made to make this a near-spiritual gathering.

Augusta National/Masters cofounder **Clifford Roberts** *ruled the roost for CBS-TV's coverage of the Masters for many years, and he would write memos to CBS's Bill MacPhail after each tournament, giving his appraisal of that year's coverage. Following is an excerpt of one such Roberts letter, following the 1964 Masters won by Arnold Palmer, as reprinted in David Owen's 1999 book,* The Making of the Masters:

During the entire telecast on Saturday not one word was said about (Arnold) Palmer having an opportunity to become the first four-time winner of the Masters. Likewise, nothing was said about Palmer having a chance to tie or better the all-time tournament record score established by Ben Hogan in 1953. Not a word was uttered about Palmer's opportunity to tie or better the 7 stroke winning margin established by (Cary) Middlecoff in 1955.

I believe it was approximately 10 minutes from the time the telecast began on Saturday until a scoreboard was shown to the viewers which gave them an accurate picture as to how matters stood, and this of course is something we have discussed in the past as being of paramount importance at an early period in each show . . .

I was informed after the show ended on Saturday that CBS had taken the precaution to tape Palmer's play of the last four holes. That being the case, it seems a pity that the producer or director failed to run off early on Saturday his playing of the last three or four holes. It would have been necessary, of course, to first explain Palmer's domination of the tournament and the records he had an opportunity to match or to break. It was approximately 38 minutes after the start of the program that (Chris) Schenkel said something about a tape of Palmer in action. Palmer was then shown at Hole No. 16 only, but the viewers must have been confused because Palmer's action at No. 16 was interrupted after he had hit his tee shot in order to show something live on another green. About four minutes afterward, the camera went back to the 16th green to show Palmer holing his putt.[26]

Steve Eubanks, *author of* Augusta: Home of the Masters
Tournament, *found in researching his book that Augusta
members can be very gracious and sociable in off-the-cuff con-
versations, but pull out a tape recorder and/or pen and pad, and
suddenly you can hear a pin drop:*

The interesting thing I found out is that everybody you
deal with on a one-to-one basis, whether a member at
the club, someone in town, or an employee or an ex-
employee or whatever, they are the nicest people you'd
ever want to be around. But as a collective group, they
are extremely closed mouth and closed door. That was a
bit ironic. As for the people in town, regardless of
whether or not they've ever been out to Augusta
National or picked up a golf club, they know where the
bread is buttered in that town. They know why they're
on the map and why people in Podunk, Idaho, know
Augusta, Georgia. They do whatever it takes to protect
the interests out there. You don't find many people in
that town speaking ill of Augusta National, and those
that do usually do so only because they've seen that long
arm stretch in their direction one too many times.

The thing that surprised me more than anything in
doing my book is the depth to which factual information
about Augusta is kept from you. For example, I did a column the year after the book came out about Bill Gates's
not getting into the club (as a member). I used a reference with one of the members who was invited to get
in—a local orthopedic surgeon. And they went nuts.
(One club official) called and went ballistic because I
had actually printed this new member's name, even
though it was fact that the guy had gotten in. It's facts

like that which are no big deal yet they are treated like national security secrets. The club doesn't tell you anything—they don't tell you how many members they have, who they are, or anything about the club itself. If it relates to the golf tournament, they may or may not talk about it.

It's a carryover from the days when Clifford Roberts ran things with such an iron fist. That sort of mentality has permeated. Granted, you have some very powerful guys who are members who want one area of their lives to remain private. And this is the one respite where they can go and not worry about news of their actions being printed (in the newspaper) or ending up in the tabloids concerning what they are doing or how much they are betting on the golf course. It's good they have a place where someone like George Schultz can go out and play a $2 Nassau with Warren Buffet, without having to worry about who's paying attention to it.

In his Augusta National–authorized book, The Making of the Masters, *author David Owen challenged an assertion that* **Steve Eubanks** *had made in his book in which Eubanks wrote that CBS's Bill MacPhail had, in effect, been used as a fall guy by Clifford Roberts when Roberts told an ill Bobby Jones that he would no longer be a part of the televised green-jacket ceremony. Owen suggested that Eubanks had no basis for reaching such a conclusion, pointing out that MacPhail had died and wasn't available to validate Eubanks's claim. Eubanks says Owen apparently wasn't aware of a meeting that Eubanks had with MacPhail before the latter passed away. Eubanks responds:*

My only concern was that Owen didn't call me. If he had, I would have told him exactly what had happened. I took Bill MacPhail to lunch at the CNN Center—we ate in a nice little Irish pub and talked for probably an hour and a half. He told me all kinds of neat stories, including the one about Bobby Jones and Clifford Roberts, and Roberts's telling Jones that it was MacPhail's decision that he would no longer be part of the telecast. It was one of many stories he told me that day. That got called into question, unfortunately, because MacPhail died. So there's no one here now to verify that this took place. I guess you could go back to MacPhail's records and perhaps find out that he did have lunch with me that day. Roberts told Jones that it had been MacPhail's decision that he would no longer be on the telecast, and MacPhail never corrected that, so he let Jones go to his grave thinking that it had been him and not Roberts who had done it.

─────

Journalist **John Derr** *has attended about sixty Masters Tournaments, starting in 1935 when he was a teenage reporter working for a newspaper in Gastonia, North Carolina, covering, of all things, the police beat:*

I went there the first time really more as an observer in 1935 than a reporter. I was just out of high school, and one of my friends for whom I had played American Legion baseball said to me one day in the middle of the week in April, "Let's go down to Augusta; they're going to have a golf tournament down there. Would you like to go?" So we drove down to Augusta on Saturday morning and bought a couple of tickets for two dollars apiece. At the time I was unfamiliar with golf tournaments to the extent that I did not know you could get press tickets.

Once I was inside I saw the desirability of being a member of the fourth estate. I had covered some football games with a couple of guys from Atlanta, including one gentleman by the name of O. B. Keeler, who was Bobby Jones's Boswell. I had covered a football game between Georgia Tech and Duke and had sat next to him. So I met Mr. Keeler and he took me around a little bit and said he would like to introduce me to some of the press. He said "There are some real nice press people here. Damon Runyan was here. Have you met Grantland Rice?" I said no, and he said, "Well, you really ought to meet Grantland Rice. Granny is a southerner and he'll help you around." So he introduced me to Mr. Rice and some of the men from New York, and Granny took a liking to me. He was very nice. I guess he recognized that I was a diamond in the rough or a real rough diamond or something. He decided that I needed help. After play was over on Saturday, Granny said, "Have you met Mr. Jones?" and I said no, and he took me over to Bob Jones.

My friend and I stayed over in a little motel Saturday night, and we watched the tournament on Sunday, and it turned out to be a very spectacular tournament. That was the day of the famous Sarazen double eagle. Nobody "happened" to be at the fifteenth hole; there were only thirteen people there. Sarazen later used to laugh about it, saying he had met twenty thousand people who claimed they were at the fifteenth when he made his double eagle there. Sarazen said, "I can name all thirteen that were there." I was at the clubhouse when it happened. The upstairs balcony was the pressroom. The reporters had their typewriters and their little tables and sat around the banisters there on the porch. Down below them sat the telegraphers from Western Union and Postal and what have you, so all the messages went out by telegram. A writer would write a paragraph or two or a little part of his story and he'd clip it to a little string and drop it over the banister. The Western Union man would pick it up and send it to the AP or wherever it was going. It was a very unsophisticated thing. All of us were out in the open and when it rained the newspapers didn't get their stories right away.

I was in that group up there on the porch when this caddie came up from down below, from out on the course, and spoke to some member of the club down below and said, "Mr. Gene had a two at the fifteenth hole." Everybody laughed because they knew he meant the sixteenth hole. The writers kept on writing their stories: "Craig Wood wins the Masters," and "Craig Wood will no longer be known as number-two Wood because he's going to win the Masters." It was about fifteen minutes before word filtered up from the course that it was, in fact, the fifteenth hole where Sarazen had holed his 220-yard shot. And he tied Wood. A lot of people claim they saw Sarazen make his double eagle. My claim to fame is that I was there and I did *not* see it. He was playing with (Walter) Hagen, and Jones had gone out to watch the last few holes and he was one of the few to see Sarazen make the shot.

I didn't stay around for the thirty-six-hole playoff. I was down there on a lark and I had to get back to

Gastonia because I was the police reporter as well as the sports reporter for the Gastonia paper. Saturday night a lot of people get locked up and you have to write about all them for Monday.

───

*Much of Derr's tenure with CBS-TV covering golf overlapped with the nearly forty years that Frank Chirkinian was at the network as its executive producer of golf. **Derr** pays his respects to Chirkinian while also recalling his later days in covering the Masters for television:*

Frank Chirkinian was the best in shutting up the announcers. He would say, "You're out here to describe it, not to be the center of it." Frank was great. And of course someone would need to shake Frank up because he was a little bit the mad dictator. The Ayatollah.

Every year we had something new. Better cables, miniaturized cameras, telephone communications. There are miles and miles of cable buried at Augusta. The players have their gurus and so do the television technicians. The year of color television was probably significant. It came in '61 or '62. I know I spent a rather sizable piece of money to have someone come to my house in Upper Montclair to adjust the color on the TV set so that my wife and daughter could watch the Masters in color. But it was with much chagrin when I came home and found out that they had watched it in black and white because they didn't want to go downstairs to see it.

One of the most exciting days of color, I did the first HDTV telecast from there. It was 1992 or 1993—the high-definition digital broadcast. The Japanese wanted to experiment with that and they got the permission from the club on the condition that I do the commentary. I did two hours of commentary every day on the fifteenth and sixteenth holes and they recorded it. They could feed that picture to a half-dozen sets that were on the grounds. There were a couple in the pressroom and a couple over in Ike's Cabin and several other places. The Sony people were there with their HDTV because they wanted to get the franchise to build that kind of set in the United States, and they had congressmen there. It was quite exciting. That is an amazing development with HDTV because you can count the legs on a bumblebee from a hundred yards. I enjoyed doing that telecast. It was good because there were times in there when play was delayed. I was able to tell a lot about what was going on.

My daughter wanted a copy of the tapes I did for HDTV, so I spoke to the producer in Japan and asked for a little tape of about fifteen or thirty minutes out of one of the eight hours I had done so that she could see the telecast and hear it. He said that he would get it over. But he didn't, so I wrote him again and one day here comes this great big package with eight hours of television, beautiful television for which you need to have an HDTV set to look at it. And they had erased all of my commentary and put in Japanese. Things that go wrong in the night.

❦

The first time writer **Melanie Hauser** *went to Augusta to cover the Masters was in 1984, and the rude awakening came when she found out that women reporters were about as welcome in the clubhouse as mosquitoes. Augusta's version of southern hospitality in those days extended to only one gender:*

My first Masters was a great experience. I remember it was cold and wet, and over and above everything else it caused me to take some action to get women reporters into the locker room at Augusta. We were not allowed inside the locker room area—not even the hallway or anything because it was attached to the men's grill. I had been looking for some amateur golfers from the University of Houston, and I couldn't go in to find them. They wouldn't even open the door to let me look inside the men's grill area or the locker room area. So I pressed my nose against the glass, and I remember a security guard laughing at me, and I remember telling him, "Don't ever laugh at somebody for trying to do their job." At that point, there was another woman reporter here, Helen Ross, and she and I talked about it and then took it to the Golf Writers' Association of America (GWAA). The following year, we were allowed into the men's grill and the locker room area. There was no discussion about it; it was just done. It was one of those things that you sort of expected for Hord Hardin to put his hand up and say, "Whoa," but he didn't at all. He just said, "Well, you're right."

Back then there were only black waiters in the clubhouse. Whether or not there was actually prejudice then, there was at least the look of prejudice at the club. Of course I knew that women were not members—just the old southern style—after all, I was raised in Texas—I'm aware of all that. I chose to go the route of Helen and I took it to a very respected member of the GWAA, and we told him what we thought. A lot of people didn't even know that. It didn't even dawn on them that women couldn't go in there because there weren't that many women covering the Masters. Little did they know that there wasn't a women's bathroom in the pressroom, either. I used to go in the men's bathroom late at night. We figured there would be a lot of discussion over that and there was none at all. When it was brought to the member, he said, "You're right. Women should be allowed. It's no problem. They'll be allowed to use the men's grill."

The next year I was in there having lunch, and (golf writer) Tim Rosaforte was sitting with me, and a man introduced himself—a friend of Clifford Roberts—and he said he wanted to shake my hand, and he said that my being there would have been something that Clifford would have believed was right. He was very, very nice about it. Then the very next day I went in there by myself and nobody would wait on me. I had to grab a waiter and say "I'm ready to order now," and it became a very uncomfortable situation. It was very much related to what blacks must have felt trying to cross the line back in the fifties and sixties in the South. After I spoke up and said I wanted to order, it was never a problem again. You did expect there would be some resistance, but there never really was any, and I applaud Hord Hardin for that because that would have been the time to say, "Ah, I don't think so."

⚬⚬⚬

In 1990 Augusta officials built a large press facility to house the many print reporters who needed ample workspace, but before then, print reporters had to make do in a two-story Quonset hut that was about two steps up from a phone booth. **Melanie Hauser** *remembers:*

The old pressroom was a Quonset hut and there was an upper deck to it. We called it the Attic and everyone up there called themselves the Attic Rats. They were really crammed in, and it was a great place up there. I was down on the bottom, and we teased that we were the Aristocrats down on the bottom. I was an honorary Attic Rat for some reason, and there was a little wave that they had. I still have an Attic Rat T-shirt from there and a picture of a bunch of Attic Rats taken from in front of the flagpole.

Then there was pressroom moderator Dan Yates calling all the women in the pressroom "pretty little ladies." "Now we have a question from the pretty little lady." It's part of Augusta. I don't know how many women over the years have come up and asked me, "Doesn't that offend you?" or to say that they've been truly offended. One woman last year (1999) was really offended and got somebody up in arms and got them to talk to the Yates brothers. But like it or not, it's part of Augusta, and they weren't saying it because they were just trying to demean women—that's just the southern way. No, it's not politically correct in this day and time, but it's part of Augusta, just like the green soles on the bottom of the caddies' shoes or the jumpsuits they wear.

It's just a unique place about which we complain from time to time, but it's something you don't ever want to miss. I missed one because they weren't credentialing Internet writers that year and that was the year that Norman fell apart (1996). I watched it on TV, and as brutal as it was watching it on TV, I can't imagine how brutal it would have been being there. Augusta is somewhere you really want to be because of the little quirks and because of the differences and the peculiar little southern ways which still exist—some of them are good, some of them bad. I dare say that no one goes to Augusta just for the Krispy Kremes. You go there to experience something that's in a different world. You can tell it from the crowd. In the early part of the week, they get a lot of people just cruising to see who's there, and it's a feeding frenzy at the pro shop. Then when the tournament starts on Thursday, it's a different crowd. You feel a difference. Where else could you put a stool down at eight in the morning by the eighteenth green and come back at one in the afternoon and nobody's moved it? This goes on all the time at Augusta, and how refreshingly wonderful it is that people still do honor things like that. Look at the crowds at Brookline for the Ryder Cup—they were out of control, just like they had been there for the U.S. Open in 1988. Face it, Boston and Philadelphia are tough towns to have a big event in, but you can't conceive of anything like that happening at Augusta.

I've seen the entire place change, from the Quonset hut thing to the huge auditorium they have for the media now, and then there's the pro shop that does millions of dollars of business. People laugh and say it will never be the Cadillac Masters. Well, it doesn't have to be that because that Masters logo itself is the sponsor of the tournament. Look at the international fans spending tens of thousands of dollars in the pro shop. It didn't used to be that way. It has always been a wonderful place, but it was more intimate back in the eighties. I can only imagine what it was prior to that. It has grown from a situation where no women were allowed in the men's grill, blacks were only waiters and caddies, and blacks couldn't handle money except to give it to a cashier that was white. Now there are female black security guards taking money in the men's grill.

Golfer **Doug Sanders** *has long been known as the peacock of professional golfers, mixing and matching colors to great effect and notoriety. It was at Augusta that Sanders first got the inspiration to include his underwear in coordinating the color of his wardrobe:*

This was many years ago when Sean Connery had just come out with 007. I was playing in Augusta and hit two really good shots to number ten on Thursday. I was wearing maroon. A week later on a Tuesday I get a letter from this guy in which he says, "Dear Mr. Sanders, I come to Augusta religiously to see what colors you wear. You were wearing maroon, which is one of my favorite colors, and you hit two magnificent shots to number ten, and when you bent over to line up your birdie putt, I could see the top of your white shorts. How uncouth can you get? Signed, 007."

The shirt I had was a mock turtleneck shirt-sweater. It did not go down into your pants, and when you bent down it could easily rise up a little bit and someone could see the top of your shorts. I told my wife about this, and so she bought like thirty or forty pairs of socks and shirts, and she sent them over to this company in San Antonio. Whenever they dyed the shirts, they would put the socks and shorts in there to have the same color as the shirts. So I'd have reds, magentas, greens, purples, and everything. And I remember one year coming back from Japan, the last thing packed on top of my suitcases was all my underwear, and I had every color you could think of. I'm coming through customs in San Francisco. This guy starts unzipping my suitcase and starts pulling the top up, when he says, "Do you have anything to declare?" And when he finished pulling the top up, he saw all my different colors of underwear. He shoved the top back down, zipped it right back up, and told me to go right ahead. I don't know if he thought I was going to ask him for a dance or what. Ever since then I've always had colored underwear to match my clothes where I've gone. Jimmy Demaret was a guy who was kind of my idol.

———

Veteran sportswriter **Dave Kindred** *paid his first visit to the Masters in 1967, and he remembers his first day there like it was yesterday:*

It was one of the great moments of my sportswriting life. I was working for the *Louisville Courier-Journal,* and I wanted to go to Augusta for two reasons: I wanted to see Red Smith and I wanted to see Ben Hogan. I walked into the Quonset hut that was the press "barn" as we called it.

And when I checked in I asked the woman in charge where Red Smith sat, and she said, "He's right over there." It was something like the third row back on the right side where he had one of those big stand-up typewriters that they must have supplied because you couldn't carry it around—it must have weighed as much as an anvil. There was Red Smith rolling a piece of paper into his typewriter, and I was a happy guy. Then I went to find Hogan, and I found him on the range. I still remember just standing there watching him. He was hitting balls that every time followed this majestic arc then fell about two yards to the right and bounced at the caddie's feet. In those days they had caddies out there catching the balls. I remember seeing Hogan's hands and noticing how thick and strong they were—they reminded me of my father's. My father was a carpenter.

That year on the third day, Saturday, Hogan shot 66. He was fifty-five years old, I believe, and he shot 36-30. We were sitting in the pressroom and on TV we could see Hogan making birdie, birdie, birdie, and finally someone said, "We ought to be out there." I watched Hogan come in. I sat in the little bleachers that they provided to the press to the left of the green at eighteen. I can still see Hogan standing over his last putt—he needs to make about an eighteen- to twenty-footer downhill for a birdie that I think would have tied the course record on the back nine—30—and it took him forever to draw the putter back, but he did and made the putt, of course, and that put him close to the lead. Clearly, it was going to be the last time he would be in contention at a major tournament. He could barely walk. He limped up the eighteenth fairway to this amazing applause, everyone standing, this little guy dragging himself up the hill.

Then afterward he sat in the locker room in the clubhouse. I don't remember what the press arrangements were at the time, other than they brought them down to the Quonset hut and we must have talked to him there, but I don't remember that. I vividly remember being in the clubhouse where he went to change shoes afterward. He's sitting on a contraption in which the shoes went under the bench, and he's on the bench with his back to a window with a white-laced curtain. The sun was coming in through the window, creating a halo effect around his head. He was the happiest guy you've ever seen, beaming at what had happened that day. There were maybe a dozen of us standing around talking to Hogan or listening to him. I don't remember anything he said; I just remember I have since gone back and looked at what I wrote. One of the things I wrote was his saying that he didn't think he could win, but that he would give it everything he had. He shot 77 the next day and fell out of contention.

What I also remember is that all of us were standing and he was seated, and at one point I looked over my shoulder to a bench in the opposite corner. There, listening to this and tying his shoes, as much in awe of this as anyone else, was Arnold Palmer. Palmer was the biggest name in the game at the time, but no one was talking to Arnold Palmer and Palmer wasn't talking to anyone, either. He was listening to Hogan.

There's kind of a P.S. to that story. Twenty years later I was working for the *Atlanta Constitution* and on the Wednesday of Masters week I've got nothing to write. Here it was 1987, and it suddenly dawned on me that it's the twentieth anniversary of the first time that I went to Augusta. That made it the anniversary of Hogan's 66. So I wrote a column basically telling about this story. Three months later I got a letter from Fort Worth, Texas, and it was Hogan thanking me for bringing back the warm memories of that day. I told my wife that day I got a letter from Ben Hogan and she said, "Who's that?" I said, "Dear, that's like getting a letter from God." Hogan was one of my heroes as a kid because I paid attention to golf and he was the guy, and he never disappointed me.

Curt Sampson took a little more than a year to research and write his book The Masters, *and he spent a good part of that time as a part-time Augusta resident:*

I traveled there a week a month for a year, so in a small way I could become a part of the community. I made some really good friends, two or three guys that I can look up whenever I go back. It's a manly hug situation. Besides just being there, I tried to eat breakfast where some of the local gossips eat, and maybe gossips is a bad word. I tried to drink where I might meet some members and I did. I just made the effort to be on the scene. Their local libraries are good. The people are generally helpful. What's striking is the disconnect between the town and the club, so totally separate for the most part. A good analogy is Rome and the Vatican—there's this little private country that is in this town but not necessarily of it.

I was assuming a very high level of knowledge by the readers. These are embers that have been kicked over innumerable times and appear every year in *Golf Digest* and *Golf* magazine before the tournament starts, and then there is the TV coverage of the very same holes and the very same club year after year. I tried to go as much as possible with original research. Big deal. I think anybody would if they could.

Sampson *also discusses the reaction he got to his book* The Masters:

Overwhelmingly positive is the short answer. The thing about club members is that they're just not supposed to talk to people like me. They don't want to be quoted— it's a condition of membership, in fact, that they don't talk to people like me. The club has very definite spokesmen—this is part of the very effective control policy. That said, I'm told secondhand that a number of members who read the book learned quite a bit. The club itself—I sent them a copy, and they asked for another and then another, and I think I ended up sending them six copies. So that's one indication, I think, that they were interested in the book. One member said through an intermediary to "Tell your friend that he should get his facts straight." So my question in return was, "Which fact? Where did we get this wrong?" He said he couldn't say. *Oh, okay, that's very helpful.*

Near the end of his book Augusta: Homes of the Masters Tournament, *author* **Steve Eubanks** *takes the club to task for not having had a sense of stewardship in the world of charities. Three years later, Eubanks was seeing a change for the better in that regard:*

One kudo I want to give Augusta refers to the last chapter of my book, *Do the Right Thing,* in which I took them to task a little bit for donating zero to charity, whereas the PGA Tour was making all sorts of donations to charities to the tune of tens of millions of dollars a year. I said to come out and do the right thing—take a portion of your proceeds and do the right thing. And they did! Here they are now the leading spokespeople out in front for the First Tee program. They were part of the formative process. They were the people standing out there with George Bush and Earl Woods at the launch of that thing, so they've been extremely instrumental in getting that project off the ground and for continuing to support it financially. I don't think I was instrumental in getting them to do that, but I think after a number of years they came to the realization finally that they needed to do the right thing. And they did.

Don't forget: Augusta National doesn't tolerate "mobs," as suggested in this notice, written in 1967, that appears on the pairings sheets given to patrons every day:

Message from Robert Tyre Jones (1902–1971) President in Perpetuity, Augusta National Golf Club:

In golf, customs of etiquette and decorum are just as important as rules governing play. It is appropriate for spectators to applaud successful strokes in proportion to difficulty, but excessive demonstrations by a player or his partisans are not proper because of the possible effect upon other competitors.

Most distressing to those who love the game of golf is the applauding or cheering of misplays or misfortunes of a player. Such occurrences have been rare at the Masters, but we must eliminate them entirely if our patrons are to continue their reputation as the most knowledgeable and considerate in the world.

Notes

1. Clifford Roberts, *The Story of the Augusta National Golf Club* (Garden City, N.Y.: Doubleday and Company, Inc., 1976), p. 13.

2. Ibid., p. 30.

3. Arnold Palmer with James Dodson, *A Golfer's Life* (New York: The Ballantine Publishing Group, 1999), p. 120.

4. Roberts, pp. 39–40.

5. Herbert Warren Wind, "The 1968 Masters: Rule 38, Paragraph 3," reprinted in Herbert Warren Wind's *Golf Book.* (New York: Simon and Schuster, 1971), p. 168.

6. Roberts, p. 114.

7. Peter Dobereiner, from a 1976 *London Observer* column excerpted in *The Making of the Masters*, by David Owen (New York: Simon and Schuster, 1999), p. 22.

8. Jack Nicklaus, with Ken Bowden, *My Story* (New York: Simon and Schuster, 1997), p. 143.

9. Peter Jacobsen, with Jack Sheehan, *Buried Lies: True Tales and Tall Stories from the PGA Tour* (New York: G. P. Putnam's Sons, 1993), pp. 195–96.

10. Roberts, pp. 103–104.

11. Nicklaus, with Bowden, pp. 15–16.

12. Wind, pp. 176–77.

13. John Feinstein, *The Majors: In Pursuit of Golf's Holy Grail* (Boston: Little, Brown, and Company, 1999), p. 114.

14. Ibid., p. 110.

15. Wind, p. 116.

16. Thomas Boswell, *Strokes of Genius* (New York: Doubleday and Company, 1987), p. 24.

17. Ibid., p. 37.

18. Herbert Warren Wind, writing in 1984 in the *New Yorker* about his first trip to the Masters in 1947, as reprinted in *The Making of the Masters: Clifford Roberts, Augusta National, and Golf's Most Prestigious Tournament* by David Owen (New York: Simon and Schuster, 1999), pp. 98–99.

19. Palmer, with Dodson, p. 118.

20. Nicklaus, with Bowden, p. 93.

21. Ibid., pp. 15–16.

22. Palmer, with Dodson, pp. 157–58.

23. Boswell, p. 40.

24. Feinstein, p. 121.

25. Ibid., p. 112.

26. Clifford Roberts, writing in 1964, as reprinted in *The Making of the Masters: Clifford Roberts, Augusta National, and Golf's Most Prestigious Tournament* by David Owen (New York: Simon and Schuster, 1999), p. 00.

Other Books Used for Background Research

Eubanks, Steve. *Augusta: Home of the Masters Tournament.* Nashville, Tenn.: Rutledge Hill Press, 1997.

Sampson, Curt. *The Masters: Golf, Money, and Power in Augusta, Georgia.* New York: Villard, 1998.

INDEX

ABOUT THE AUTHOR

Mike Towle is a veteran sportswriter and author whose previous books include *True Champions* and *The Ultimate Golf Trivia Book*. A former newspaper reporter, he has covered golf for the *Fort Worth Star-Telegram* and *The National*. He has also written numerous articles for *Golf World*, *Golf Shop Operations*, *Golf Journal*, and *Golf Illustrated* magazines. Towle is president and publisher of TowleHouse Publishing Company, based in Nashville, Tennessee, where he lives with his wife, Holley, and their son, Andrew.